5.98

MODEL THEATRES

And How to Make Them

MODEL THEATRES

And How to Make Them

Alan J. Allport

William Luscombe

First published in Great Britain in 1978 by
William Luscombe Publisher Limited
The Mitchell Beazley Group
Artists House
14–15 Manette Street
London W1V 5LB

ISBN 0 86002 115 7

Set in 11/13pt Century Schoolbook
by Tradespools Ltd., Frome, Somerset.
Printed in Great Britain by
Morrison & Gibb Ltd.,
Edinburgh.

CONTENTS

INTRODUCTION

The desire to make models is inherent in most of us: model ships, soldiers, trains and aircraft roll off the kitchen table production-line in many households and will no doubt continue to do so for many years to come. Psychologists can, perhaps, explain this inborn desire to make miniatures, but for most of us it simply provides an interesting hobby which gives hours of enjoyment. Moreover it is harmless!

For the origins of the model theatre we have to go back to the early nineteenth century, to one of the most colourful periods in history when the Peninsular War was at its height and Bonaparte was doing his best to keep Josephine at arms' length: the Americans were trying to annexe Canada to the annoyance of the British who were trying to stop them. About this time it dawned on some enterprising artist that there would be a ready market for portraits of the theatrical 'giants' of the day, in monochrome or colour – not single illustrations but four to a sheet and all characters from the same play. The sheets would be suitably captioned and beneath each drawing would be the actor's or actress's name and the part he or she was playing. One of the most successful artists of the day was Robert Dighton and it is believed that he was the far-sighted originator of this lucrative idea.

Dighton's sheets were so popular that four drawings to a sheet soon grew into six and from six it was an easy and logical step to illustrate all the characters from a play, often showing the principals in several changes of costume and posture. The characters alone were only part of the story and before long sheets of scenery were added, usually of a backcloth and wings, all faithfully representing the original stage production of the play. The earliest preserved toy theatre sheets however, were not published by Dighton, but in 1811 by a gentleman called William West, and it is generally assumed that it was West who laid the foundations of the toy theatre, or, more accurately, of the 'Juvenile Drama'. West was a man of tremendous industry who published well over 140 sheets of plays during his lifetime. He was also a man of taste, commissioning first class artists to do the drawings and adopting only the very latest printing techniques. His sheets were minor works of art, some of them reproducing in miniature the proscenium arches of prominent London theatres and often including the instructions and paraphernalia needed to produce special scenic effects.

Most of the sheets available at this time could be purchased in black and white ready for colouring or already hand-coloured – hence the expression 'Penny plain, twopence coloured', a catch-phrase that will for ever be associated with the toy theatre.

West prospered, but like many of his kind, became too ambitious and when he extended

Little Red Riding Hood

his activities into the pornographic book trade – which existed even in those days – his business gradually declined and he ended his days a pathetic and lonely man. However, the tradition which he had established lived on and the cult of the Toy Theatre spread to France, to Germany, to Denmark and to the United States where the firm of Scott and Co. of New York published *Selty's American Boys' Theatre*. One of the most popular American productions was splendidly entitled *The Fiend of the Rocky Mountains*. German character and scenery sheets were particularly elaborate, often hand-coloured and invariably three or four times larger than their British or American counterparts. Understandably, their most popular plays were *Hansel and Gretel*, *William Tell*, *The Flying Dutchman* and *Lohengrin*. Instructions were often printed in English, French and German, and many such sheets were exported to Britain where they enjoyed great popularity.

The middle years of the nineteenth century bought with them the 'penny dreadful' – popular stories, published in weekly instalments at a penny a time and including sheets of characters or the scenery for a well-known play. Competition in this field was fierce and publishers were forced to reduce production costs by using cheap, thin paper and rough, often indecipherable printing. Many of the plays offered were of a crude and flamboyant character which did not find favour with the moral, non-conformist Victorian age. Also the pace of life was increasing, thanks mainly to the invention of the internal combustion engine: new techniques were being developed, new hobbies discovered and gradually the popularity of the toy theatre declined. In fact it might have died completely but for a small number of enthusiasts among whom we find none other than Robert Louis Stevenson, of *Treasure Island* fame. His article 'A Penny Plain and Twopence Coloured' in a popular magazine did much to revive the flagging interest in the toy theatre. It is, in fact, due mainly to the efforts of Stevenson and like-minded enthusiasts that the toy theatre has survived to the present day and it is a curious fact that most of those on sale at our major stores still follow almost exactly the style and decor of the 'penny plain, twopence coloured' of a century ago.

Nowadays interest in the toy theatre is fostered and maintained by, amongst other things, exhibitions; by the formation in 1925 of the British Model Theatre Guild and by the enterprise of a select band of devotées including Mrs Margaret Fawdry and The Pollock family whose Toy Theatre Shop and Museum in London's Scala Street is a Mecca for all toy theatre lovers. From here it is possible to purchase, in book form, a complete model theatre, including the scenery, characters and text for a wide variety of plays. The list of 'notables' who have owned model stages is impressive. Amongst them we find the names of W. S. Gilbert, Ellen Terry, R. L. Stevenson, G. K. Chesterton, John Gielgud and the young Winston Churchill whose gift for rhetoric was probably born on the boards of a model stage.

This then is the background to the model theatre of today. In such an outline I have not been able to dwell, for example, on the work of Hodgson, Skelt, Webb, Redington or Pollock – all great names in the saga of the toy theatre. The story of the Pollock family alone, and its association with Mrs Fawdry, is well worth a chapter to itself. To anyone wishing to delve more deeply into the story of these remarkable people, and many others, I thoroughly recommend George Speaight's splendid book on *The History of the Toy Theatre*.

My main purpose in writing this potted history as an introduction to the more practical matters to come is to awaken enthusiasm for a most fascinating subject, and to show would-be modellers that they are carrying on a great tradition.

The teacher wishing to foster an interest in drama, or the 'hobbyist' with theatrical leanings will find that building a model stage and presenting a play, however simple, will give expression to that romantic strain which is usually present in even the most sober members of our community. Whatever your age, a model theatre is fun to build and operate.

CHAPTER 1
THE MATERIALS YOU NEED

What you need to make a start: advice on selecting cardboard, glue, paint and other basic requirements

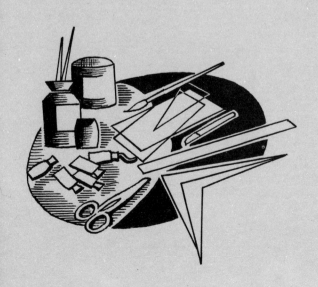

It is quite possible to make a rough-and-ready stage model out of an old cardboard box – I've made dozens in my time – but, if you intend to make a really decent model, it is worthwhile spending a little money on materials and equipment.

Cardboard

The basic material is, of course, cardboard. I usually buy a few sheets of mounting board in two thicknesses, say around $\frac{1}{16}$ in (1·5 mm) and $\frac{1}{8}$ in (3 mm) in white, fawn, red and brown. You can choose almost any stiff card, including those smooth-surfaced boards used by artists for pen and ink work, or water colour boards which have a rough or 'toothed' surface. However I recommend mounting board simply because it is softer in texture than any of these others and much easier to cut and to 'score'.

You will also need a few sheets of brown, black and white paper, but you don't have to buy them all at once. Get them as you need them – otherwise you could waste an awful lot of this rather pricy material.

Working Surface

I would advise you to set aside a sheet or even a couple of sheets of the thicker board as a working surface, unless, of course you happen to be one of those fortunate people with an old table whose top you can carve up to your heart's content!

Glue

Your second basic requirement is a good reliable glue. It is almost impossible to choose one type of glue to suit all purposes and my advice to you is to use one glue for small surfaces and another for the larger areas. In both categories the choice is wide. My personal preference for small surfaces is Croid No. 1.* It is a very strong, clear liquid glue which I have found to be very satisfactory indeed for sticking wood, cardboard, leather, paper, glass and most other materials, except certain plastics. If you have difficulty in obtaining it, other clear adhesives are just as good.

For larger surfaces you can use the old tried-and-trusted office glue or one of the many rubber solution adhesives available. I find rubber solution adhesives excellent, but be warned – they are highly inflammable so do be careful.

Rulers

Next on your list should be an 18 in (45 cm) ruler (also marked in centimetres) and a pen-knife. There is a great deal of cutting and 'scoring' to be done using the ruler as a

---

* The products I mention by name in this book I can recommend from personal experience. There are, however, many other similar products available throughout the world, which are equally effective. Choice is often a matter of personal preference. The important thing is that they work for you.

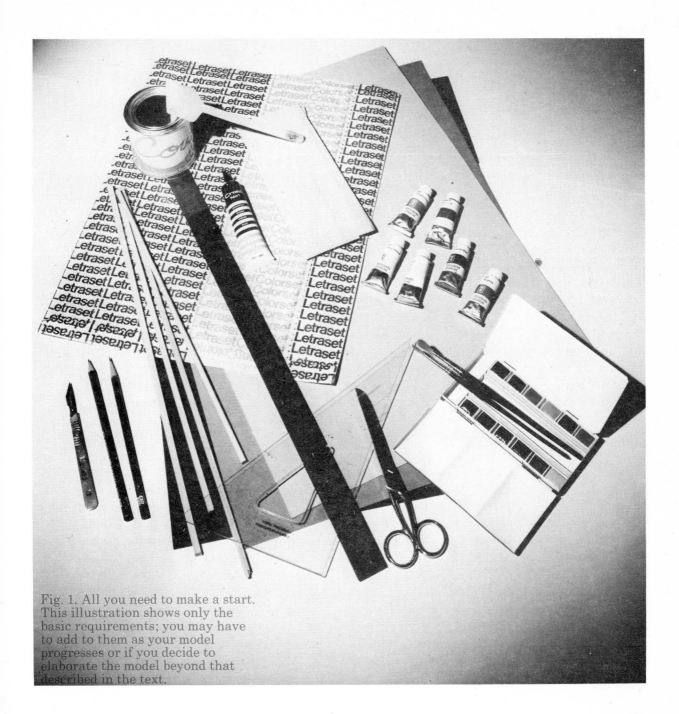

Fig. 1. All you need to make a start.
This illustration shows only the
basic requirements; you may have
to add to them as your model
progresses or if you decide to
elaborate the model beyond that
described in the text.

straight edge and it is all too easy to cut into the wooden or plastic variety, so ruining both ruler and penknife. For that reason I always prefer to use a metal ruler.

Knives
A good knife with a really sharp blade is essential. It can be an ordinary penknife providing the blade is sharp, but for most purposes I prefer to use a scalpel similar to those used by surgeons. The advantage here is that you can buy one handle and any number of detachable blades. When the blade edge is dulled from constant use it can be detached and discarded and a new blade fitted. If you decide to use a scalpel, do so with great respect. They are exceptionally sharp and one slip can make a nasty mess of your hand.

If you have an old, blunt knife by you, don't discard it. You will find it very useful for 'scoring' a surface before bending.

Wood
Although the model will be built mainly from cardboard, there are some parts which are much stronger if constructed from strips of wood. For this purpose a few lengths of $\frac{1}{4}$ in (6 mm) square strip are ideal. Later on you may need an assortment of balsa wood, to use when making scenery. This is a very soft wood, easy to cut and shape with your knife or by light rubbing with a fine sandpaper or emery cloth.

Paints
When we start building scenery and 'making' the actors you will need water colour paints and brushes. You can, of course buy a box of students' water colours, but I would advise you to purchase small tubes of gouache or poster colour. A very wide range of bright colours is available and they have the tremendous advantage of drying flat. Don't fall into the trap of investing in a large collection; you can get by very well with red, blue, yellow, black and white for a start. You can add more exotic colours as you need them. When buying brushes, by the way, get the best you can afford. It is often said that to buy cheap is false economy and this is particularly true of brushes. Start with a couple of decent sable brushes, say sizes 4 and 7. You can add to them later if necessary.

Letrafilm
As an alternative to paint you may prefer to use one of the 'instant' products like Letrafilm which is made by Letraset. Such products are much used in advertising studios. Letrafilm consists of a range of adhesive film in 119 different colours. It is heat resistant and transparent and you can draw or paint on its matt surface. It or similar products can be bought from most stores selling artists' materials. You will find such film particularly useful when building scenery. I prefer it to coloured papers, though admittedly it is a little more costly. Sketches and instructions

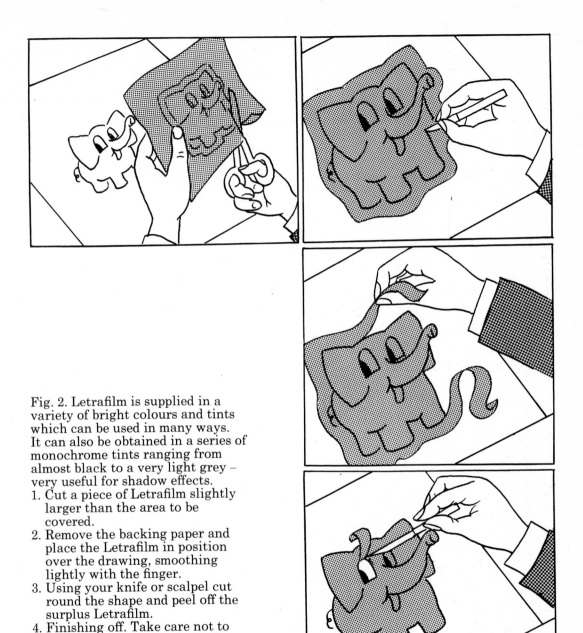

Fig. 2. Letrafilm is supplied in a variety of bright colours and tints which can be used in many ways. It can also be obtained in a series of monochrome tints ranging from almost black to a very light grey – very useful for shadow effects.

1. Cut a piece of Letrafilm slightly larger than the area to be covered.
2. Remove the backing paper and place the Letrafilm in position over the drawing, smoothing lightly with the finger.
3. Using your knife or scalpel cut round the shape and peel off the surplus Letrafilm.
4. Finishing off. Take care not to cut too deeply particularly if you use a scalpel. They are very sharp and could cut right through the card.

13

on how to use Letrafilm will be found on page 13.

'Specials'

As we progress you may find a need for 'special' material – braid for the front curtain for example. This will depend very much on how far you want to go with your model and how elaborate you want it to be.

Incidentally I have refrained from mentioning pencils and erasers. These will certainly be needed. Use a fairly soft (grade B) pencil, by the way; it's much easier to rub out than the hard (grade H) variety. Yet another small but useful item is a set square.

And that is quite sufficient equipment with which to make a start.

A brief note about tracing: I find the best method is to trace in pencil onto thin paper. Turn the paper over and scribble on the reverse with a soft (B) pencil. Turn the paper right side up, place it onto the thin card, and draw over the figures again with a hard (H) pencil. You will get a very satisfactory image.

CHAPTER 2
THE STAGE

How to construct the
foundation of the model:
designing and constructing
the proscenium

The stage platform

This is the foundation of our model and it must be well and solidly constructed.

Take one of the pieces of the thicker white card and mark out the plan shown in Fig. 4 Diagram A on page 18. Use your set square to check the right angles. The dimensions suggested will give you a finished model of around 18 × 15 × 15 in (46 × 38 × 38 cm). If this is too large you will have to adjust the dimensions proportionately.

Scoring

Scoring is simply the marking of the surface with a blunted blade to make folding easier. This is all very fine when working with paper or thin board but when scoring thickish card – as at present – your penknife or scalpel will give a better result. The great secret of successful scoring is to maintain even pressure, otherwise you will get an ugly 'broken' fold. This will require some practice as it is very easy to score too much or too little. Only from constant practice will you learn just how much pressure to exert. Too little pressure is not serious as you can always go over it again, but if you are too heavy-handed you may cut right through the card and you will have to start again, or try to patch up the platform with tacky tape. Don't forget, by the way, to do all your cutting and 'scoring' on the cutting surface mentioned in the chapter on Equipment.

Having 'scored' the lines to your satisfaction, bend along them as shown in Fig. 4 Diagram B, and glue the four side flaps (1. 2. 3. 4.) as indicated. Take a sheet of thick card size 18 × 15 in (46 × 38 cm). This is the base board to which you must glue the stage platform as indicated in Fig. 4 Diagram C. When you are satisfied that the glue has set and you have a good firm platform base, cover the top surface with fawn coloured paper, using Cow Gum or similar rubber solution adhesive for the purpose. Incidentally when using rubber solution adhesive be careful to follow the instructions on the tin. These will probably tell you to spread the 'gum' thinly on both surfaces before bringing them together. The 'gum' is actually a contact adhesive and it is advisable to leave each coated surface for a few minutes before fixing. One of the major advantages of such an adhesive is that any surplus glue which has managed to get where it is not wanted – and it often does – can be removed with an eraser or even with the fingertip.

The proscenium

The evolution of the proscenium arch is not without interest: for its origin we have to go right back to those rather splendid amphitheatres so popular in Greek and Roman times. Originally these were divided into the *auditorium*, the *orchestra* and what they called the *scene*. The actors appeared only in the orchestra area. The next step was the intro-

Fig. 3. Here is your model stage as it would be seen from a seat in the dress-circle. Note the effective use of the gold fringe trimming on the curtains. It is these little touches which add realism to your model.

17

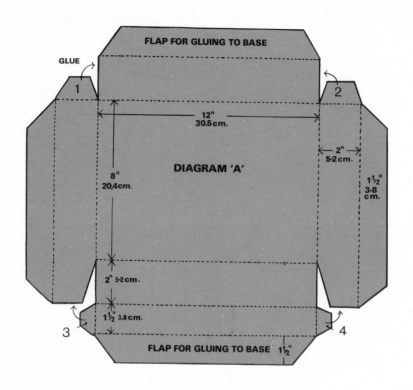

FLAP FOR GLUING TO BASE

GLUE

1

12"
30.5cm.

2

8"
20.4cm.

DIAGRAM 'A'

2"
5·2cm.

1½"
3·8
cm.

2" 5·2cm.

1½" 3.8 cm.

3

4

FLAP FOR GLUING TO BASE 1½"

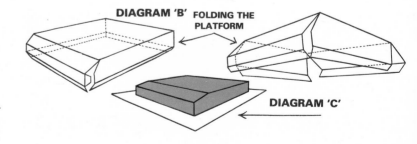

DIAGRAM 'B' FOLDING THE PLATFORM

DIAGRAM 'C'

Fig. 4. Extra care must be taken in preparing the base. If this is not correctly and accurately constructed it will be difficult to fit the backstage superstructure on it, and you may have some minor but irritating problems with which to contend.

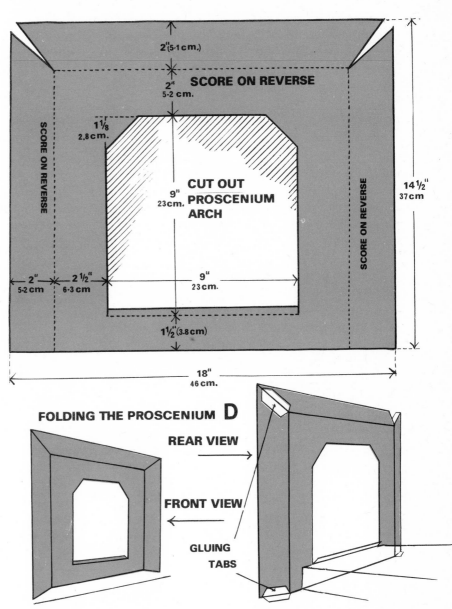

2"(5·1 cm.)

2"
5·2 cm.   **SCORE ON REVERSE**

1⅛
2·8 cm.

SCORE ON REVERSE

9"
23 cm.   **CUT OUT
PROSCENIUM
ARCH**

SCORE ON REVERSE

14½"
37 cm

2"
5·2 cm   2½"
6·3 cm

9"
23 cm.

1½" (3·8 cm)

18"
46 cm.

FOLDING THE PROSCENIUM D

REAR VIEW →

FRONT VIEW
←

**GLUING
TABS**

Fig. 5. The instructions 'score on reverse' may be confusing but if you will turn back to Fig. 3 you will see how this operation works in in practice. The two lower illustrations will also help to guide you.

19

duction of a raised acting area called the *proskinion* from which our word 'proscenium' is presumably derived. The so-called *scene* was used only as a background and as a form of rest area for the actors.

In due time stage designers realised that the *scene* was a very suitable area in which to exercise their talents and they began to cover the backgrounds with decorative motifs appropriate to the play. It was standard practice to allow five exits from the acting area, the central exit being an archway through which the distant countryside could be seen. The desire for more space prompted designers to widen this central archway and to use the area thus created as additional acting space. This development reached its logical conclusion during the seventeenth century when the entire action of the play took place *behind* the archway. The archway itself was curtained off from the auditorium and orchestra, and what the Romans called the *scene* had thus evolved into what we call the proscenium.

It is an odd fact that having pushed the stage behind the proscenium arch, the designers should eventually decide to bring it forward again – thus we now have the projecting stage and the even more advanced arena stage in which the audience is seated, usually in tiers, around the acting area. Not unlike Greek and Roman amphitheatres, you

may say: and you would be right. In fact, in theatre design we seem to have come 'full circle'.

In my opinion the proscenium stage offers greater scope than its modern counterparts for model making and puppetry. That is why, in this book, I have concentrated on making a model of the proscenium stage.
And so, back to our model . . .

Take a sheet of fawn coloured cardboard and mark out the proscenium as indicated in Fig. 5 on page 19. Cut out the complete shape, including the proscenium arch, and 'score' as shown. Note that the scoring in this case is on the reverse side. Fold the sides and top inwards as shown in Fig. 5 Diagram D.

At this stage you should carry out whatever decoration you choose on the proscenium arch. On the illustration (Fig. 3) of my model on page 17 I have simply stuck coloured panels on the sides and top. The frieze above the arch was drawn on white paper and glued onto the panels.

Having completed your 'decorations', cut out two small tabs and glue them on the reverse and at the top of the proscenium. You will also need similar tabs at the base (see Fig. 5 Diagram D). Finally glue the proscenium to the base board and to the stage platform.

CHAPTER 3
BACKSTAGE

How to construct and fit the 'tormentors', backcloth and wings: preparing the drop curtains and proscenium fringe

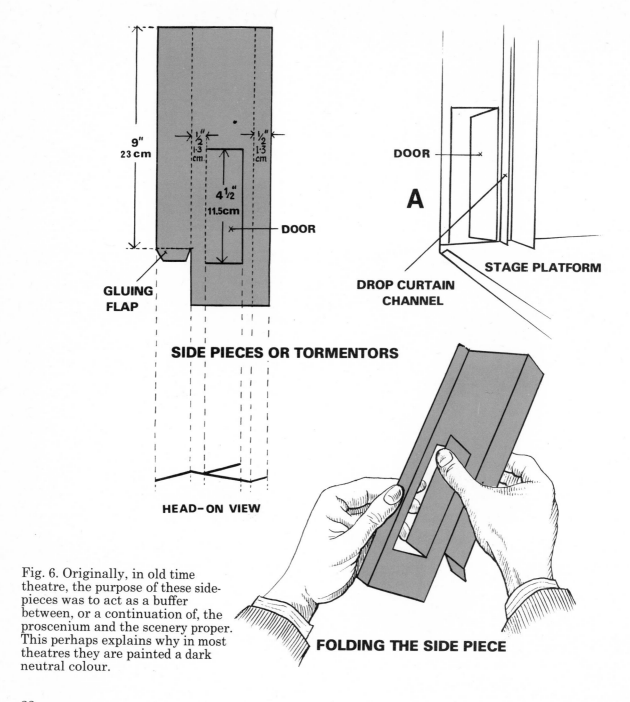

9"
23 cm

½" 1·3 cm

½" 1·3 cm

4½"
11.5cm

DOOR

GLUING
FLAP

SIDE PIECES OR TORMENTORS

HEAD–ON VIEW

DOOR

A

STAGE PLATFORM

**DROP CURTAIN
CHANNEL**

FOLDING THE SIDE PIECE

Fig. 6. Originally, in old time
theatre, the purpose of these side-
pieces was to act as a buffer
between, or a continuation of, the
proscenium and the scenery proper.
This perhaps explains why in most
theatres they are painted a dark
neutral colour.

22

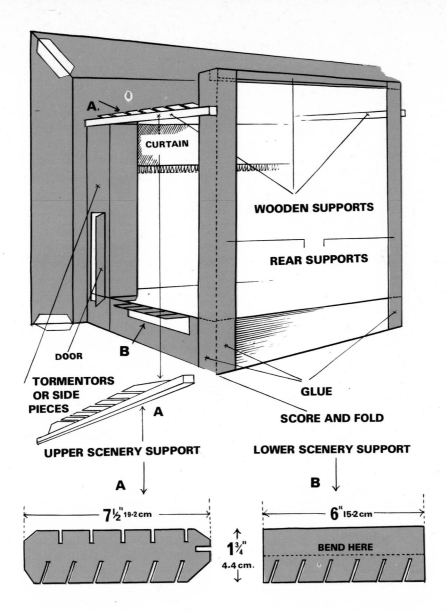

A.

CURTAIN

WOODEN SUPPORTS

REAR SUPPORTS

DOOR

B

TORMENTORS
OR SIDE
PIECES

A

UPPER SCENERY SUPPORT

GLUE

SCORE AND FOLD

LOWER SCENERY SUPPORT

A ↓

B ↓

← 7½" 19·2 cm →

1¾"
4·4 cm.

← 6" 15·2 cm →

BEND HERE

Fig. 7. This diagram shows only one
method of fixing the 'backcloth
and wings' type of scenery. It is
perfectly satisfactory for most
model stages, but, providing the
wings are firmly anchored top and
bottom, you can use any method
you choose to keep them in place.

Going backstage in a real theatre is a fascinating experience, particularly for anyone who likes to find out what actually makes things happen. There is a bewildering maze of ropes, pulleys, flats, drops, lines, spots and other items too numerous to mention. Accordingly our model has, of necessity, to be very much simpler than the real thing – though it is amazing what can be achieved with a combination of imagination and ingenuity.

Everyone concerned with the production will be on hand to see that nothing goes wrong with his or her particular job and to deal with those last minute crises which always seem to happen seconds before 'curtain up'.

The size of the modern stage does not allow much room for manoeuvre: it usually occupies rather less than one third of the depth of the auditorium. It was the limitation of floor space backstage that forced designers to introduce various mechanical and electrical devices in order to make the best use of what space they had. Most of these devices came originally from Germany and included sliding stages, sinking stages and revolving stages. A particularly ingenious device was the double elevator stage, installed in a New York theatre in 1888.

Although the more sophisticated contrivances were developed during the nineteenth and early twentieth centuries, the Romans, centuries earlier, had their backstage problems too and we learn from the writings of Pliny the Elder, of two wooden theatres, built in 50 BC which revolved on pivots so that they could be used separately in the mornings and rolled together to form an amphitheatre for the afternoon performances. Maintaining the two sections in good running order must have given the stage manager – or whatever he was called in those days – several king-size headaches. What happened, we wonder, when the wood warped?

Fortunately no such catastrophe is likely to happen to us, but we cannot expect to complete our model without running into some snags. Let us hope that they will be minor ones!

Side Pieces

We will start with the side pieces, known as *tormentors*, which are the two supports behind and on either side of the proscenium. They are substantial units and each has an access door or curtain to allow actors or stage staff to appear before the drop curtain. These tormentors are quite tricky to make so please study Figs. 6 and 7 carefully before you start chopping up your precious cardboard. Cut out the complete section, including the door, score and fold as indicated. Cover the outer side with a neutral paper, grey or brown preferably, and glue each tormentor into position as indicated in Fig. 6.

Drop Curtain Channel

This is not absolutely essential but I think you will find it very worthwhile. In order to make a channel into which the drop curtain can easily slide, you should glue $\frac{1}{2}$ in (1·25 cm) strips of brown card to $8\frac{1}{2}$ in (21·5 cm) lengths of $\frac{1}{4}$ in (6 mm) square wood and glue them onto the inside of each door. Fig. 6 will, I hope, explain this to you more clearly than words. Remember that accuracy is important.

Rear Supports

After these two rather difficult operations comes an easy one – the two supports at the rear and on either side of the platform. These are, quite simply, two pieces of thick card, 1 in (2·5 cm) each way, scored and folded down the middle and glued at each rear corner. See Fig. 7.

Side Supports

Take the $\frac{1}{4}$ in (6 mm) square length of wood and cut two 10 in (25·5 cm) pieces. (Cutting can be carried out with your knife or with one of those miniature hacksaws which can still be bought at most 'Do-it-yourself' or model shops.)

Glue these lengths firmly in position on the outside and at the top of the side and rear supports (see Fig. 7). One further length of 12 in (30·5 cm) should now be cut and glued across and on the outside of the rear supports – again see Fig. 7.

Wing Supports

I shall tell you in a later chapter how to make complete scenery units which can slide into position. But you will almost certainly need to use backcloth and wings scenery and we must therefore make certain that this type of scenery can easily be accommodated when necessary. The backcloths (or drops) need support only at the top, but I have always found it advisable to support wings (or flats) at top and bottom – they are easily fouled by the 'actors' if not firmly fixed.

Sketches A and B in Fig. 7 are, respectively, the top and bottom supports. Copy them onto a medium thickness card, cut out and bend as shown. You will, of course, need two of each – one set for each side.

They must then be glued onto the wooden battens on either side of the platform. The illustrations in Fig. 7 show clearly the positioning of these supports, but do make certain that top and bottom are in line. Otherwise your wings will be all askew with disastrous results.

You have now almost completed the backstage. What remains is the all-important drop curtain and proscenium fringe. In my model I have used plain dark red cardboard with a golden fringe which I bought at a local store very cheaply. I found that the material stuck quite easily to the cardboard.

25

If you are following my suggested dimensions, the drop curtain will be about 12 in ×
10 in (30·5 × 25·5 cm). Before fixing the fringe,
however, make certain that the curtain fits
easily between the side pieces.

Now, if you have managed to follow me so
far, you will have the skeleton, as it were, of
your model stage, all ready to tackle the
fascinating subject of scenery. Before doing
so, however, we ought to provide an orchestra.

Is this the smallest model theatre
in the world? It fits into a
matchbox!

CHAPTER 4
THE ORCHESTRA

Composition of a modern orchestra: the strings, woodwind, brass and percussion: the conductor: Some advice on tracing

The Orchestra

An orchestra is not usually required during the run of a straight play, but sometimes 'canned' music is used to establish the mood of a play or to provide a little light diversion during intervals. I think our model, however, ought to have an orchestra – even if only a small one.

It is interesting to note that in the ancient Greek theatre the *orchestra* was the space between the auditorium and the proscenium.

It was here that both the actors and instrumentalists were stationed. In fact 'music' for the Greeks meant not only music in our sense of the word, but literature and artistic activities generally. They made their music with a number of instruments with strange sounding names. Most of us have heard of the lyre, but how many of us have ever come across the *cithara*. Yet this was a popular instrument, much in favour with professional musicians. Then there was the *tibia* – not, as you may think, the shinbone – but a sort of oboe which was in regular use in Roman times. One instrument which crops up consistently, whatever the period of history, is the flute. Greek, Roman, Renaissance or modern times, whatever else may fall by the wayside, the flute trills merrily on. It is a sobering thought that even as far back as 311 BC the flute players of Rome went on strike, presumably for a few more sesterces an hour! They took themselves off to a neighbouring town and resumed work only after most of their demands were granted!

The modern orchestra usually consists of four main sections – string, brass, woodwind and percussion.

Strings

To many people strings mean violins, but in fact the violin family consists of a number of instruments with similar characteristics but differing substantially in tone. These are the viola, cello, the violin itself and the daddy of them all, the double-bass. In a really large orchestra there can often be more than thirty first and second violins – the difference refers merely to the parts played and not to the instruments themselves. Other instruments within the string family are the harp, mandolin, piano and, of course, that instrument so beloved by modern youth, the guitar.

The Brass

This category embraces the horns, trumpets, cornets, trombones and tubas. Brass is in fact something of a misnomer as some of these instruments can be made of silver, copper, horn or even wood.

The Woodwind

Some musicians regard the woodwind and the brass as two divisions of wind instruments but for our purpose I prefer to treat these divisions separately. The difference between them mainly is that the woodwind covers those instruments in which the sound is made through cane or air reeds. In brass the sound is made by the vibration of the lips against the mouthpiece. Woodwind instruments are flutes, clarinets, oboes, saxophones and bassoons. This latter instrument is a powerful fellow capable of making its presence felt in any orchestra. Also in this section you may find recorders and bagpipes if they are needed for some special purpose.

The Percussion

For many people this is the most fascinating part of an orchestra. There cannot be many of us who have never been stirred by the 'rum-tum-tum of a military drum'. But in addition to the various drums (kettle, side, bass) this section keeps an eagle eye on a whole range of instruments and gadgets such as triangles, cymbals, castanets, gongs, rattles, bells, dulcimers (glockenspiel) and xylophones, not to mention tambourines and any number of special effects such as the cannon used to such purpose in Tschaikovsky's 1812 overture!

We cannot hope, in the space at our disposal, to have a full orchestra in our model theatre but I suggest we build one as follows:

Tuba, Trombones (2), Trumpets (2), French Horn, Flute, Clarinet, Bassoon, Oboe, Violins (4), Cello, Double-bass, Harp, Piano

Percussion: Kettle-drums, side drum, triangle, tambourine, tubular bells, whistles, fireworks and a whole variety of 'noises off'

To keep all these musicians in order we shall, of course, have to give them a conductor.

The accompanying sketches (Figs. 8 and 9) are all actual size. Copy or trace them onto thinnish card and then colour them to your choice. The men will certainly be wearing dinner jackets, but you can make the two ladies as glamorous as you like.

Cut out the figures in groups as shown, then cut short pieces of $\frac{1}{4}$ in (6 mm) square wood and glue them to the bases of the figures.

All the orchestra now needs is something to keep its high spirited members in place, so we must construct a barrier as indicated in Fig. 9. See also the photograph (Fig. 3) on page 17. Place the members of the orchestra in position as shown in Fig. 9, and add the barrier. The stage itself is now complete.

HARP 1 **PIANO 2** **TYMPANI 19** **DOUBLE-BASS 3**

CELLO 4 **FIRST VIOLINS 5 & 6** **SECOND VIOLINS 7 & 8**

FLUTE 9 **BASSOON 10** **TRUMPET 11** **TROMBONE 12 FRENCH HORN 13**

Fig. 8. There has always been some controversy, even as far back as the eighteenth century, as to the true position of the orchestra in the theatre. Is it a part of the auditorium or of the stage? Or is it a separate section on its own? What do you think?

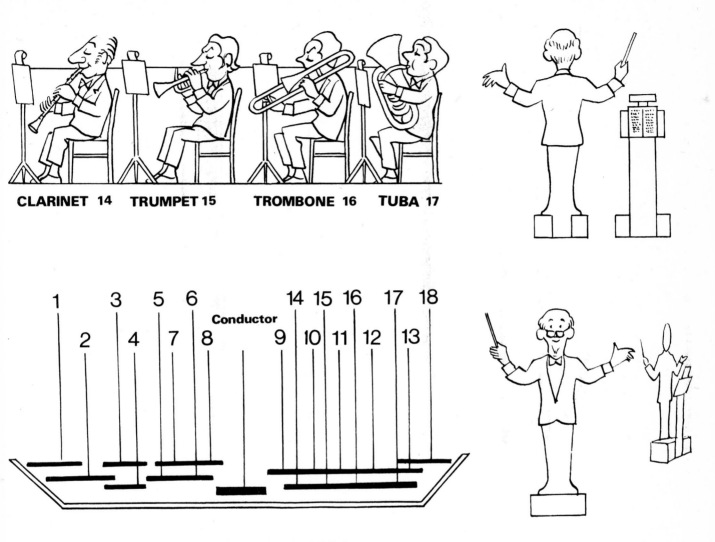

CLARINET 14 TRUMPET 15 TROMBONE 16 TUBA 17

POSITIONING THE ORCHESTRA

Fig. 9. The rest of the orchestra with the conductor. His job is to weld together all the separate instruments into one complete whole. He should be familiar with the performance of each instrument and able to present the listener with a well balanced musical score.

CHAPTER 5
SCENERY

Some background notes:
ingenious special effects:
building a 'box' set: how to
enlarge a drawing by the
'square' method

Much has been written about stage scenery by specialists in a wide variety of books. The subject is an enormous one and I can touch on it only briefly here, but if you like to delve a little more deeply into the history, or evolution of stage design and scenery I can recommend *Designing and Making Stage Scenery*, a Studio Handbook by Michael Warre, with a foreword by Peter Brook.

Another excellent two-volume book is *Twentieth Century Stage Decoration* by Rene Fuerst and Samuel Hime, published by Dover Publications Inc. of New York. *Volume 1* traces the evolution of stage design during this century and *Volume 2* is given over almost entirely to illustrations. The authors have gone to considerable trouble to give a truly international flavour to the book and the illustrations cover work by most of the more important scenic designers in Europe and America. In fact, in addition to the United States, fifteen European countries are represented and the range of design from the simple to the complicated is quite staggering. But these photographic illustrations cannot show the ingenious devices which, over the years have been adapted by impresarios, to fool, to mystify and to entertain the audience. And remarkable effects they must have been. For example, by using a system of folding flaps, operated by stage hands, scenes could be changed instantaneously 'before the very eyes' of the audience. Lavish use was made of

trap doors and I still remember vividly, as a small boy, sitting entranced through a scene in which a member of the Lupino family successfully eluded the clutches of two demons by leaping, with astonishing agility through a succession of trap doors cunningly built into the scenery.

Fire, fog, rough seas, transformation scenes (by using gauzes and transparent material lit from behind) were engineered by early designers in the face of incredible difficulties. More recently, theatrical spectaculars have featured, amongst other things, the sinking of a pleasure liner, a crashed aircraft, and, incredibly, an earthquake.

You may like to exercise your ingenuity and produce similar(!) special effects on your model stage later on. Initially, let us confine ourselves to the simpler and more straightforward forms of scenery. Before getting down to detail, however, I must explain that the sides of the stage are usually referred to as Prompt and Opposite Prompt (O.P.). Facing the auditorium the left side is Prompt and the right side is O.P. It is the opposite in the U.S.A.

Now let us start with the most elementary or basic form of scenery. This consists of wings (or flats) together with backcloths or drops. An extension of this simple form is the addition of 'borders' above the stage from wing to wing and 'return flats' – additional flats hinged to the wings and set at an angle to them.

Figs. 10 and 11 show the stage fitted with a backcloth and wings – the latter designed to slot into the supports described in Chapter 4.

This elementary form of scenery is ideal for the model stage as it allows ample room in which to manoeuvre our 'actors'. Designing and building elaborate sets with staircases, pillars and rostrums, is great fun, but making your miniature performers mount a flight of stairs or leap from rostrum to rostrum can be a tricky business!

The Box Set

The other main form of scenery is known as the 'box set'. As the name implies, this consists of a box – square, rectangular, triangular or multi-sided, with one side open to the audience. When making a box set I usually include a suitable flooring so that the scene is complete in itself and can be positioned on the stage at a moment's notice – much quicker on a model stage than fixing backcloths and wings.

Fig. 12 shows a typical box set and how it would be positioned on stage.

The instructions given so far in this chapter are of a very general nature. But they should have been sufficient to show that when designing scenery there are practically no

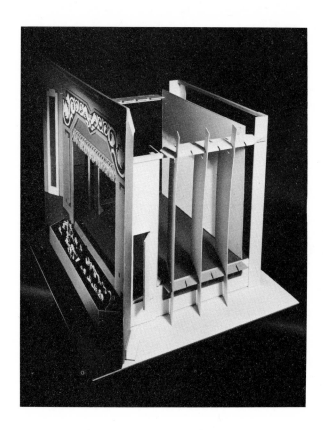

Fig. 10. The complete model with 'dummy' backcloth and wings in position. Note the Tormentors through which the actors – or actresses – can make an appearance when taking a bow in front of the drop curtain.

limits to the enterprise and ingenuity of the imaginative designer. It is unfortunate that our model cannot be adequately lit. Lighting plays an important – even an essential part in any theatrical production. The experienced designer frequently gets an atmosphere across by clever use of lighting. And talking of atmosphere it is vital that the scene should reflect the mood of the play. One would not, for example, design similar sets for, say, *The Sound of Music* and *Hamlet*!

But before we get down to designing the settings for a specific play, let us look at some of the methods of preparing the scenery.

Square Enlarging

I have found that old illustrated calendars can provide plenty of material for backcloths. Sometimes the size fits perfectly, and all you need to do is to mount the illustration on suitable card. More often than not, of course, you will have to enlarge it from a small illustration – or *vice versa*. Many of you may have sufficient draughtsmanship to tackle this sort of job, but if not study Fig. 13; this shows how to use the square method for copying or enlarging. This is a foolproof technique which I used for many years with great success. Just as an example I decided to enlarge the sketch at the top of the page by one third. So I marked off the sketch in $\frac{1}{4}$ in (6 mm) squares both vertically and horizontally. Then I repeated the 'grid' below, but making

$\frac{3}{8}$ in (9 mm) squares: it was then a simple matter to copy the original, square by square, and, as you can see, the reproduction is surprisingly accurate.

Incidentally the design illustrated in Fig. 13 provides, with its two wings, a very satisfactory woodland scene, particularly if you colour it with paint or with Letrafilm.

Another method of reproduction is by using the simple copying technique described in the previous chapter.

Yet another method is to call in the assistance of your photographic friends – unless, of course, you are a photographer yourself. Very often, an atmosphere can be achieved by building a scene entirely from black and white photographs: an even more dramatic effect can be obtained by using sepia-toned prints and picking out the highlights in white paint.

One could go on indefinitely, talking about scenery and suggesting many different ways of preparing settings, but I must leave you to use your ingenuity in devising whatever effect you need. In the meantime I propose to give you my ideas for some of the scenery and characters for three of the best known plays in the English language – *The Merchant of Venice, Romeo and Juliet*, and *A Midsummer Night's Dream*.

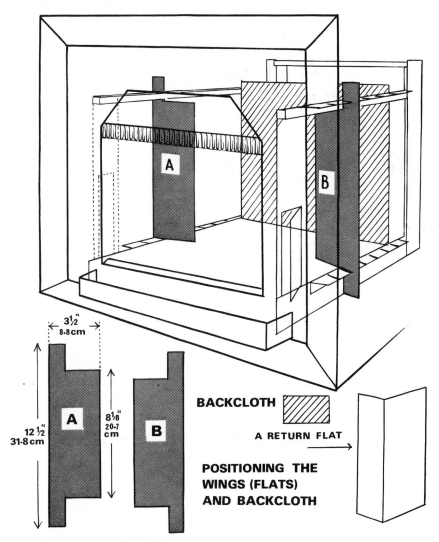

BACKCLOTH

A RETURN FLAT

POSITIONING THE WINGS (FLATS) AND BACKCLOTH

FLATS (WINGS)

$3\frac{1}{2}''$
8·8 cm

$8\frac{1}{8}''$
20·7 cm

$12\frac{1}{2}''$
31·8 cm

A

B

Fig. 11. Fixing the simple 'backcloth and wings' type of scenery. You can, if you wish, stretch a strip of material from the top of wing A to the top of wing B. This is a useful 'ploy' if, for example, you want a woodland scene in which the trees meet overhead.

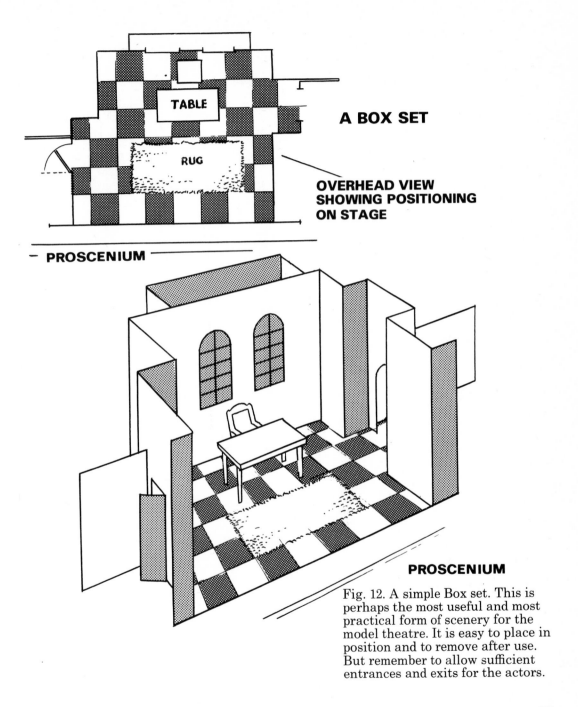

A BOX SET

TABLE

RUG

**OVERHEAD VIEW
SHOWING POSITIONING
ON STAGE**

PROSCENIUM

PROSCENIUM

Fig. 12. A simple Box set. This is perhaps the most useful and most practical form of scenery for the model theatre. It is easy to place in position and to remove after use. But remember to allow sufficient entrances and exits for the actors.

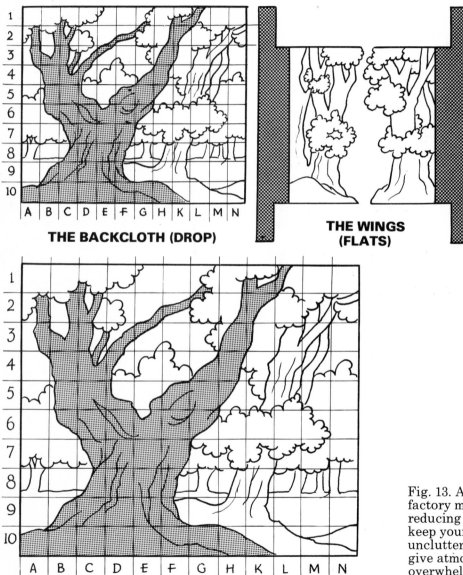

THE BACKCLOTH (DROP)

THE WINGS (FLATS)

Fig. 13. An easy but very satisfactory method of enlarging or reducing an illustration. Try to keep your designs simple and uncluttered. They are intended to give atmosphere to a play, not to overwhelm or dominate the actors.

CHAPTER 6
SETTING
A PLAY

The Merchant of Venice

Setting the scene: designing
and constructing the scenery:
the story and characters:
perspective in stage scenery:
an illusion of depth: shadows
and highlights

The Merchant of Venice was written by William Shakespeare sometime between 1594 and 1596, about the same time as he wrote those other great comedies *The Taming of the Shrew* and *A Midsummer Night's Dream*. Besides being a literary genius, Shakespeare was himself no mean performer on the stage. He worked originally in a theatre in Shoreditch and in 1598 he had a considerable hand in leasing a plot of ground near London's Bankside at Southwark, where the Globe theatre was founded. As a playwright, Shakespeare blended his unique powers of characterisation with a remarkable understanding of every side of human nature: nowhere is this more manifest than in *The Merchant of Venice*.

In a book of this nature I cannot hope to take you through the whole of the play. What I propose to do is to set out a few ideas for some of the best scenes. I will, of course deal with the well-known court scene in some detail.

My copy of *The Merchant* indicates that the play is set (somewhat naturally) in various parts of Venice; at Portia's house and in a Court of Justice. So, for a start, here is a design for *A Street in Venice*.

Those of you who haven't had the good fortune to visit that elegant city may have formed the impression that Venice is com-posed entirely of canals and lagoons linked by the occasional bridge. But there are, in fact, charming little backwaters and quite substantial squares – and most certainly there are streets. I have visualised one of them in Fig. 14. This is basically a simple triangular box set, drawn in line, with strong shadows introduced with the aid of Letrafilm.

Copy this design, using the 'squares' method to increase the size to the given dimensions. Apply grey Letrafilm to the shadows and cut out the highlights with your scalpel. Score as indicated (the centre score is on the reverse) and bend as shown in Fig. 14 Diagram B.

I strongly recommend the addition of a crazy-paved or cobbled floor and if you want to add a little colour to the scene, stick to yellow and blue as marked on the sketch.

When using this set, place it fairly well back on the stage to allow the 'actors' room to enter and exit from either side in front of the scene.

A Public Place
Another scene which occurs more than once in my copy of the play is *Venice – a public place*.

There's nothing more public in Venice than St Mark's Square, and if you stand in the

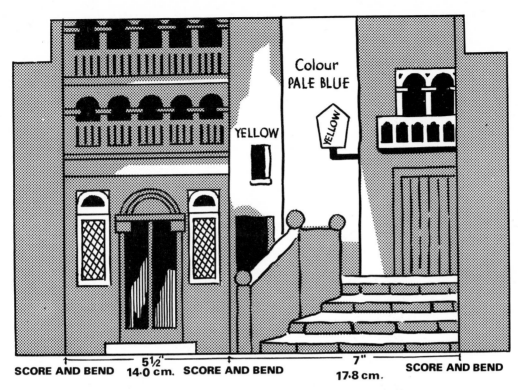

Colour
PALE BLUE

YELLOW

YELLOW

SCORE AND BEND   5½"   SCORE AND BEND   7"   SCORE AND BEND
                14·0 cm.   17·8 cm.

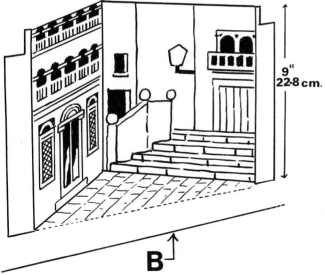

9"
22·8 cm.

B

SCENERY FOR A
STREET IN VENICE

OVERHEAD
VIEW

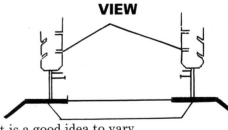

Fig. 14. It is a good idea to vary
your scenery as much as possible.
This not only allows you to
exercise your imagination, but
helps to maintain audience interest.
This simple scene is a good example
of the two-sided box set.

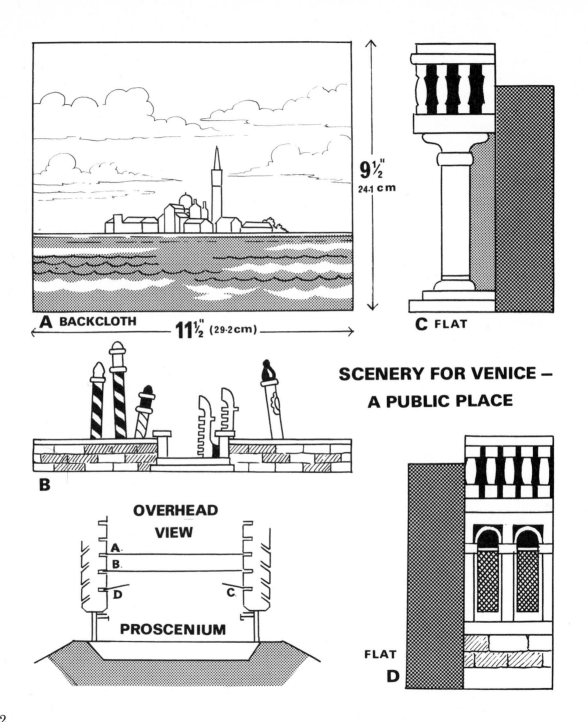

A BACKCLOTH

9½" 24·1 cm

11½" (29·2cm)

C FLAT

B

SCENERY FOR VENICE –
A PUBLIC PLACE

OVERHEAD
VIEW

A.
B.
D   C.

PROSCENIUM

FLAT
D

Piazzetta where the Doges Palace meets the waterfront you look across the Pool of St Mark's towards the church and monastery of the Island of St Georgio Maggiore. This seemed to be a most suitable backcloth for Venice – a 'public place' indeed – and Fig. 15 Diagram A shows this beautiful island in a much simplified form. Enlarge this sketch to the required size and colour it either with gouache, watercolour or with Letrafilm.

In this scene it is necessary to interpose a break between the lagoon and the piazzetta, so in Fig. 15 Diagram B I have sketched out a low wall incorporating some of those attractive multi-coloured posts which serve as parking meters for unmanned gondolas. And talking of gondolas, those strange lop-sided, flat-bottomed black-painted forms of water transport are an essential part of the Venetian scene. We cannot unfortunately include a complete gondola in our 'public place' setting, so we will do the next best thing and show the distinctive bows of two gondolas moored against the wall. Make sure to get the design right – a hatchet-like head, six 'teeth' projecting outwards and one tooth facing inwards.

Fig. 15. This is a particularly interesting scene to construct because it includes a backcloth which is, in fact, a simplification of the real thing and not a figment of the imagination.

The wall should be restrained in colour, mainly browns and greys, but you can let yourself go on the mooring posts. The more colourful, the better! The gondola bows are always white. To complete the scene we have the wings, which I have kept very simple. Copy them to the necessary size, and colour them pale grey with the windows in dark blue. Here again – although not shown in my sketch – I advise a flagstone flooring.

The Story

Before we get down to preparing the characters in *The Merchant of Venice* a brief reminder of the play itself would not be out of place.

The story concerns Antonio (the merchant) from whom his friend Bassanio has borrowed 3,000 ducats in order to pay court to his girl friend, Portia. Antonio has, in turn, borrowed the money from Shylock – a wealthy Jew – on condition that if the loan is not repaid within three months, Shylock would claim one pound of flesh from Antonio's body. The loan is not repaid and Shylock demands his grisly forfeit. But Portia, disguised as a Doctor of Law, saves Antonio by reminding the Jew that the penalty does not mention blood and that, unless neither more nor less than an exact pound of flesh is cut, his life – Shylock's – is forfeited. Loud Cheers; congratulations all round, except for poor old Shylock who slinks off in disgrace – a pathetic and broken man.

The Actors

According to my copy of the play there are eighteen principle characters involved, plus Magnificoes of Venice, Officers of the Court, Servants and other attendants. In Fig. 16 I have designed and illustrated costumes for four of these characters, including Portia and Nerissa.

You can of course set the play in any period you wish, and *The Merchant* has indeed been performed many times in modern dress. I may be old-fashioned, but I prefer to keep to the period which I believe the author intended, and my costumes are based on Italian dress of the 14th century. I was able to borrow an excellent book on *Costumes through the Ages* and although I have taken some liberties, my designs are generally authentic. The important thing to remember, however, is that costumes must be theatrically effective.

If you have been working throughout to my suggested dimensions, you will find that these 'actors' are all actual size. If not, you will have to copy them by the 'square' method. Whatever size you choose the first step is to transfer them to drawing paper or card and colour them suitably.

Remember that in those far off times long hair and flamboyant costumes were the order of the day for men of quality, so do not be afraid to use plenty of strong, vivid colours.

Having coloured your actors to your satisfaction, they should be cut-out and pasted onto a cardboard backing to give them added strength.

Since I started making model theatres many years ago I have experimented with various means of introducing the characters to the stage, but I always come back to the simple and obvious method of pushing them on from the wings. Cut a strip of thin card about $\frac{3}{8}$ in (9 mm) wide and 12 in (30·5 cm) long (you can vary the length according to the size of your stage). Take an ordinary match and cut off four pieces of about $\frac{3}{8}$ in (9 mm) each. Glue these to each end of the strip of card, side by side, and with sufficient space between them to accommodate the lip on the base of each figure (see Fig. 17 on page 45).

It is necessary to have these supports on each end of the cardboard strips so that the characters can be introduced from either side of the stage.

Each strip of card should be of the same colour and texture as the scenery floor. This acts as a camouflage and makes the 'controls' less obvious. The Duke, of course, will not need a control – he can be placed in position in the court scene before 'curtain up' and he can remain there throughout the entire Act, without having to be moved.

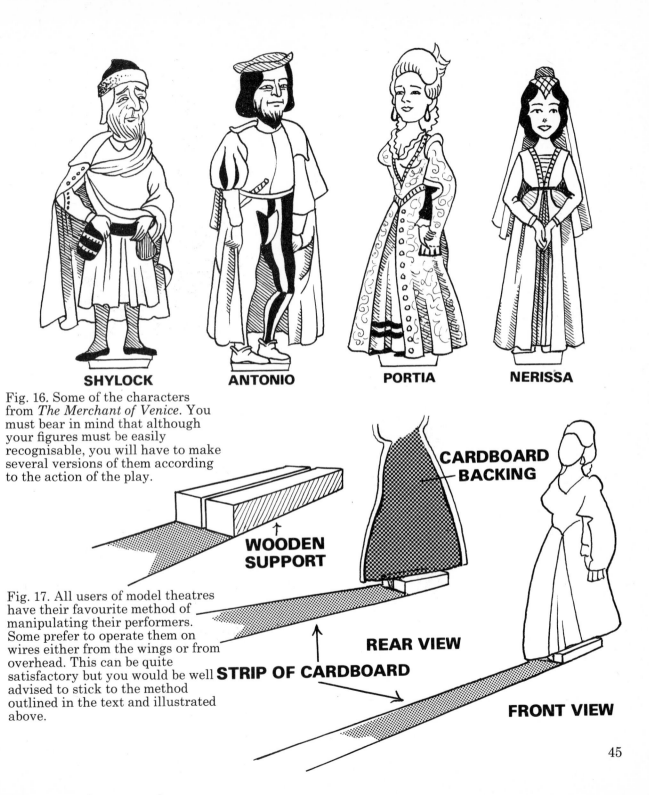

SHYLOCK

ANTONIO

PORTIA

NERISSA

Fig. 16. Some of the characters from *The Merchant of Venice*. You must bear in mind that although your figures must be easily recognisable, you will have to make several versions of them according to the action of the play.

CARDBOARD BACKING

WOODEN SUPPORT

REAR VIEW

Fig. 17. All users of model theatres have their favourite method of manipulating their performers. Some prefer to operate them on wires either from the wings or from overhead. This can be quite satisfactory but you would be well advised to stick to the method outlined in the text and illustrated above.

STRIP OF CARDBOARD

FRONT VIEW

45

A Court of Justice

Now we come to one of the best-known dramatic scenes in English literature – the tense situation culminating in the humiliation of Shylock and the triumph of justice over inhumanity.

I have made a model of this famous scene which is illustrated for you in Figs. 18 and 19. In it I have deliberately used the design to demonstrate the vital use of perspective in designing and constructing stage scenery.

The backcloth consists of dark brown simulated panelling. The throne in the centre is covered with dark red paper and there is a small overhead canopy. The Duke of Venice will sit here flanked, perhaps, by two court officials and separated from the well of the court by an ornately carved wooden screen. To set them apart from the protagonists in the trial, the Duke and his officials are accommodated on a slightly raised platform.

On either side of the throne there are windows; these are made from light blue paper and outlined in black. Next we have a pair of wings cut out of dark red card to simulate curtaining and terminating in a fringe of bronze-coloured card.

But it is to the front cloth that I must draw your special attention. In order to give depth to the scene I have used the old trick of exaggerated perspective. In very simple terms, the principle of perspective is that everything which recedes from us appears to vanish at a point on the horizon. The best example is perhaps a railway/railroad track. You know and I know that the rails are equidistant to the end of the line. But to the human eye the space between them appears to decrease until the rails merge at what is known as the vanishing point or eye-level. Objects higher than eye level appear to vanish downwards and those below appear to vanish upwards. Apply this principle to stage scenery and you will see how, by drawing the side panels and the roof in perspective the scene is given an illusion of depth.

It is of equal importance in a scene of this kind to observe shadows and highlights. I have assumed in this case that the main source of light would be high in the centre of the stage. This would throw a strong light on the lower part of each panel, while the upper section would be in shadow. On my model I have painted in the highlights with a mixture of yellow and white paint and a mixture of blue and black for the shadows. It is this treatment which helps to give a three-dimensional effect to a flat surface.

When Shylock prepares to take his 'pound of flesh' he will need somewhere to place his scales, so the scene is completed by the addition of a small table, centre stage.

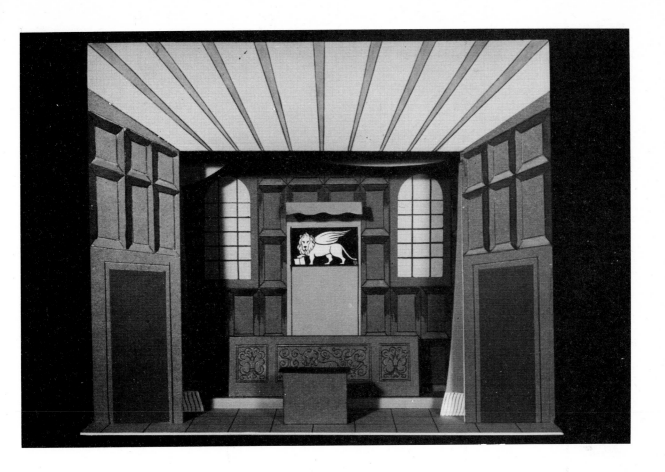

Fig. 18. The notables of Venice liked – indeed demanded – luxury, even in a Court of law. So, although the general tone of this scene should be restrained, there must be an air of quality in the panelling and furniture.

Fig. 19. The Court scene in plan, showing the positions of scenery etc.

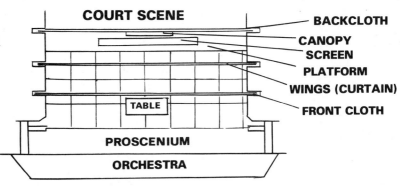

COURT SCENE

BACKCLOTH

CANOPY

SCREEN

PLATFORM

WINGS (CURTAIN)

FRONT CLOTH

TABLE

PROSCENIUM

ORCHESTRA

47

CHAPTER 7
ENTER THE PLAYERS:

A Midsummer Night's Dream

The story told simply: settings for the principal scenes; creating the characters: *Pyramus and Thisbe*

Ask any number of people to name four of Shakespeare's plays and it is more than likely that *A Midsummer Night's Dream* will be on most of their lists. Ask them to tell you the plot, however, and they will probably mutter something about Oberon, Titania, Puck and, of course Bottom. Everybody knows Bottom – the chap with the donkey's head! As for the plot itself, they usually haven't a clue and who can blame them, for it is a 'confusion' of mortals and fairies, with mistaken identities aggravated by the antics of a mischievous sprite. I will now simplify the story for you!

The play opens in the Palace of Theseus, Duke of Athens, where plans are in hand for the wedding of the Duke to Hippolyta, Queen of the Amazons. Their deliberations are interrupted by the arrival of Demetrius and Lysander, two gentlemen of the court, and Hermia with her father Egeus. Lysander eloquently pleads for Hermia's hand in marriage but Egeus has already promised his daughter to Demetrius and the Duke orders her to obey her father or be banished for ever from the court. The situation becomes even more complicated when Helena, a local beauty, confesses her hopeless love for the handsome Demetrius. But love will always find a way and Lysander's way is to flee with his Hermia to the forest, hotly pursued by the frustrated Demetrius after Hermia, and the equally frustrated Helena after Demetrius. But the road is long and the day is warm and

in due time nature takes its course and the two couples lie down to rest and sleep.

Meanwhile all is not well in the fairy world and King Oberon and his Queen are having one of those 'tiffs' which happen in even the best regulated families. In a fit of pique Oberon orders Puck, a mischievous sprite, to bring him a love juice which, when sprinkled on sleeping eyelids *'will make man or woman madly dote upon the next live creature that it sees'*. This potion is to be used on the sleeping Titania in the hope that she will awaken *'when some vile thing is near'*.

But down in the forest something stirs – it is in fact a company of workmen intent on rehearsing a performance of Pyramus and Thisbe, their contribution to Theseus' wedding festivities. Their leader is Bottom, a weaver by trade and a simple country yokel by nature.

Puck meanwhile has distributed the potion lavishly, his victims being the two young noblemen as well as the sleeping Titania.

To cap everything, he replaces Bottom's homely features with a donkey's head and it is with this strange creature that Titania falls madly in love when she awakes. Lysander and Demetrius are similarly affected, the object of their amorous advances being Helena.

In all, it is a fine old mix-up, but eventually

Oberon orders Puck to put matters right. Demetrius surrenders Hermia to Lysander and devotes his attentions to Helena and at the Duke's wedding feast – at which three marriages are celebrated – Bottom and his group of players present an hilarious rendering of *Pyramus and Thisbe*.

Scenery

I think that you will find that I have provided enough material to enable you to stage the complete play if you wish.

Most of the action takes place in *A Wood near Athens*, although in the stage directions it varies with remarkable originality from *Another part of the Wood* to simply *A Wood*. The other settings are *Theseus' Palace* and *A Room in Quince's House*. I have prepared designs for two of these scenes – *Theseus' Palace* and *A Wood* – and there is a miniature sketch which will be helpful for Quince's house. Remember that he was a carpenter and the place would be littered with the tools of his trade. Theseus' palace is a fairly spartan establishment, but there is some decoration on the two columns and marble figures in each of the alcoves. Be careful with the cutting, and particularly with the scoring which must be made on the reverse side; be sure not to cut away the two top support tabs which are needed for fixing into the scenery slots. You need not follow my design in detail but I suggest that you maintain the general pattern of central opening with forward folding sides. For this scene and the *Wood near Athens* you will need a backcloth and Fig. 20, diagram X will suit both palace and wood very adequately.

For *A Wood near Athens* I have introduced a new technique. Using a piece of brown card size $11\frac{1}{2} \times 9\frac{1}{2}$ in (29·1 × 24 cm) I indicated the tree trunks in pencil and then cut out with a sharp knife the areas between them. Then, instead of naturalistic trees I cut out a number of cloud-like shapes in green paper of various shades, and glued them onto the trunks. The result was particularly effective and I recommend you to try it. When cutting out these shapes keep the scissors steady and move the paper round them. This may seem an odd procedure but once you have learnt the trick you will find it much easier than keeping the paper stationary and snipping away at it.

To complete the scene you should place a sheet of green paper on the stage platform to represent grass.

The Characters

Figs. 23–25 provide sketches of the principal characters, with Puck about to anticipate Concorde by '*putting a girdle around the earth in forty minutes*', and also on his knees with the phial of love juice. The Fairy Queen, Titania, is also shown in two poses, pontificating in all her regal majesty, and sleeping

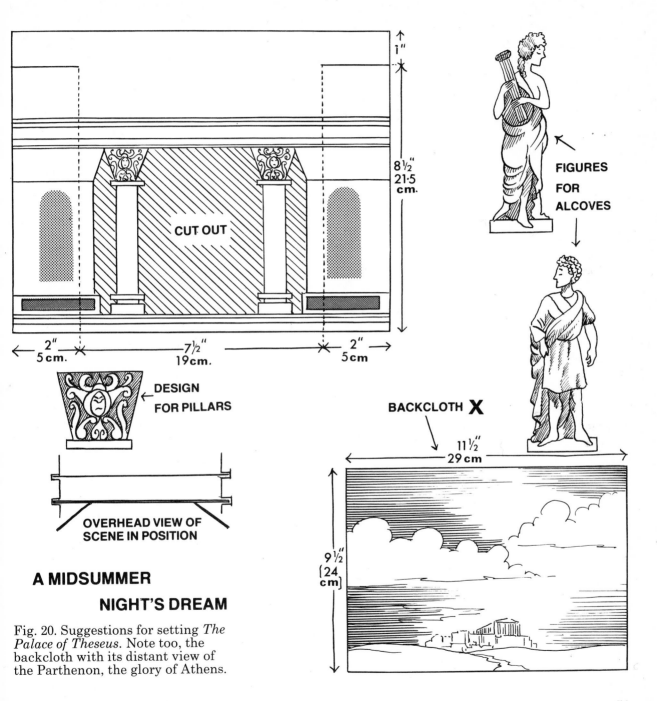

1"

8½"
21.5 cm.

CUT OUT

FIGURES
FOR
ALCOVES

←— 2" →|←————— 7½" —————→|←— 2" —→
5 cm.   19 cm.   5 cm

DESIGN
FOR PILLARS

BACKCLOTH X

OVERHEAD VIEW OF
SCENE IN POSITION

11½"
29 cm

A MIDSUMMER
NIGHT'S DREAM

Fig. 20. Suggestions for setting *The Palace of Theseus*. Note too, the backcloth with its distant view of the Parthenon, the glory of Athens.

9½"
(24 cm)

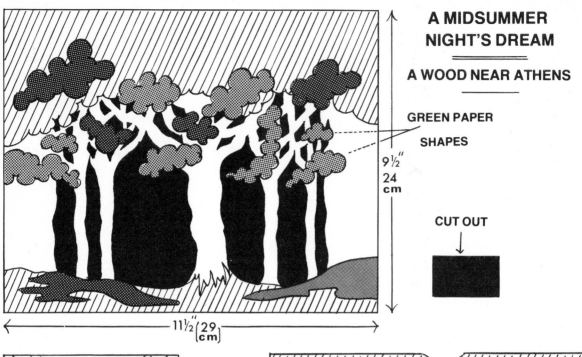

A MIDSUMMER NIGHT'S DREAM

A WOOD NEAR ATHENS

GREEN PAPER

SHAPES

9½″
24 cm

11½″ (29 cm)

CUT OUT

A ROOM IN QUINCE'S HOUSE

Fig. 21. The woodland scenes are not the easiest to achieve effectively, but the use of green paper as described in the text can be recommended.

Fig. 22. (*Opposite*) The Immortals face to face with Bottom and Company in the Woods near Athens. The orchestra, presumably, is playing music by Mendelssohn!

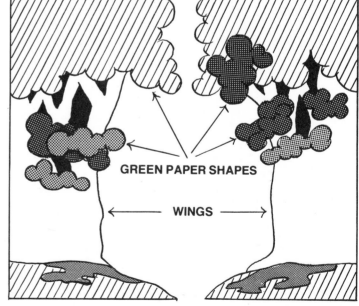

GREEN PAPER SHAPES

WINGS

innocently upon a grassy bank – fairly asking for trouble! Bottom is, of course, shown with and without his ass's head.

Trace these figures onto card and colour them appropriately. There should be a subtle difference between mortals and non-mortals: this effect is achieved professionally by the use of clever lighting but for our model stage I can only suggest that Oberon, Titania, Puck and the attendant fairies are clothed in various shades of green. By contrast you can use bright colours freely on the Duke and his court, but Bottom and his friends should be more soberly dressed, as befitting hard-working tradesmen.

The performance by Bottom and Co, is of course, a travesty of the original story! Bottom is cast as Pyramus, Flute as Thisbe; Starveling plays Thisbe's mother; Snout is a wall; Quince is moonshine and kindly old Snug tries to pass himself off as a ferocious lion. For our purpose, use the characters as already designed with the exception of Snug who you will find on page 56 heavily disguised as a King of the Jungle.

And that just about concludes my proposals for *A Midsummer Night's Dream.* So let us leave Theseus and his court to their wedding celebrations, while Bottom and his team refresh themselves after their 'triumph'.

Titania　　　**Hippolyta**　　　**Hermia**　　　**Helena**

Bottom – a weaver　　　**Bottom**　　　**Quince – a carpenter**　　**Flute – a bellows mender**

54

Oberon

Theseus

Demetrius

Lysander

Puck

Fig. 23. Helena, we are told, is a bigger girl than Hermia. Also, she is blonde and light-skinned in contrast to Hermia who has a dark southern beauty. They have the temperaments to match their colouring – Helena sweet and feminine, Hermia more aggressive and lively.

Fig. 24. Other characters from *A Midsummer Night's Dream,* including the mischievious Puck.

Fig. 25. (*overleaf*) More Mortals and Immortals, making up the most delightful and amusing cast of characters in all of Shakespeare's plays.

Snout – a tinker

Snug – a joiner

Starveling – a tailor

Titania resting

Pease – blossom

Snug – as lion

Mustard-seed

Cobweb

56

CHAPTER 8
PRESENTING
A PLAY:

Romeo and Juliet

Brief synopsis of the play: some
notes on colouring the
principal characters:
presenting them on stage

For our third ration of Shakespeare, I suggest we tackle the scene in which Juliet, unable to sleep, comes out onto her balcony and confesses her love for Romeo. This is the scene beginning with Romeo's well known soliloquy, '*But soft! what light through yonder window breaks?*'

Before making a start we ought to remind ourselves very briefly of the story. It concerns the vendetta between two leading families in mediaeval Verona – the Montagues and the Capulets. Romeo is a Montague and Juliet a Capulet, a situation which spells trouble when Romeo sees Juliet at a ball and the two youngsters fall deeply in love. Romeo pleads his cause so effectively that Juliet readily consents to be his wife and the lovers are secretly married by Friar Lawrence, an old friend of both families. Their happiness is rudely shattered when Tybalt, a nephew of Capulet, fights and kills Mercutio, Romeo's most intimate friend, in a street duel. Romeo avenges the death of his friend, but is exiled by the Prince of Verona.

The lovers are broken-hearted, but the law is the law, and in despair Romeo departs for Mantua. Being ignorant of Juliet's marriage to Romeo, her parents endeavour to force her into marriage with Paris, a close friend of the family. In despair, the unhappy girl flees to Friar Lawrence and begs for his help. The good friar gives her a potion which induces a death-like sleep. Her parents believe her to be dead and she is conveyed with solemn ceremony to the family vault. Meanwhile the kindly priest sends a message to Romeo explaining what he has done. Unfortunately Romeo fails to receive the message and on returning secretly to Verona and finding his lady-love apparently dead, himself drinks a phial of poison and collapses in agony across the body of his young wife. Slowly Juliet awakens and, in a frenzy of grief, stabs herself.

Scenery

The setting for the balcony scene is in Capulet's orchard and I have made a simple model of this scene which you may like to use as a guide. I have illustrated this both photographically and in plan form. (Figs. 26 and 27).

I suggest that you mark out the design in pencil on fairly stiff card, then go over it with black ink, finally spreading various shades of brown water colour over the walls to give the effect of mellow stonework. By the way, if you use a ball-point pen to mark out your design, make sure that the ink is waterproof. Otherwise the application of water colour will set the ink running and produce a sorry mess. One way of preventing this is to use a laundry marker pen – they have to be waterproof! The 'squiggles' on the smaller gateway are intended to represent wrought iron, but if you find this too detailed or complicated, simply fill in the area with black paint. The trees on the right are needed to give point to Romeo's reference to the moon *'that tips with silver all these fruit-tree tops'*. The trees can be whatever you like to make them; we can assume that the main orchard is hidden behind the balcony wall. We can also dispense with the moon, but you will need a backcloth and for this a piece of dark blue card is sufficient. If you *must* have a moon, cut a $\frac{3}{4}$ in (19 mm) diameter circle of yellow paper and glue it to the backcloth. The balcony is not difficult to make and if you stick closely to the design you will find that when folded it will fit snugly into position. I advise you to prepare a flooring, marked to represent flagstones, and then to glue the scenery into position on it.

It may be that you would like to stage another scene from *Romeo and Juliet* and, as a sort of bonus, I have suggested a treatment for what the text calls *Verona, a Public Place*. A great deal of the action takes place here, including much roistering and revelry, as well as the exciting and colourful duel scenes. This setting is designed in triangular box form and as with all sets of this kind you must decide how you intend to introduce your characters. If you feel that the single right and left entrances are insufficient, cut away the large arch and draw the house and garden on separate card and fix it as shown in Fig. 28, diagram X. This is intended to be the Town Gate and the building on the left is one of those taverns where the lads and lasses consumed vast quantities of whatever it was they drank in those days.

The Characters
My copy of *The Oxford Shakespeare* lists 21 principal characters in *Romeo and Juliet* plus the usual collection of citizens, musicians, pages, guards and attendants. Seven of these principals are illustrated in Fig. 29: Romeo, Juliet, the nurse, Lord and Lady Capulet, Tybalt (Capulet's nephew) and the hot-headed Mercutio, Romeo's friend. Don't be surprised to find the lovers looking like teenagers; they were both very young and, in fact, the nurse tells Lady Capulet that Juliet will not be fourteen until Lammas Eve.

Trace these characters onto card of medium thickness and colour them suitably. Use strong colours; I suggest mainly crimson, dark green, blue and gold. These people were not peasants and could afford to wear good clothes. Some of the local citizens and country folk would be roughly clothed but most of the gentry were comparatively affluent and dressed well. Romeo No. 1 is romantically dressed for the balcony scene while Romeo No. 2 is more formally attired. This could well be his costume when he first sets eyes on Juliet at a ball in Capulet's house. *'What lady is that which doth enrich the hand of yonder knight?'* he asks and this sparks off the whole tragic story.

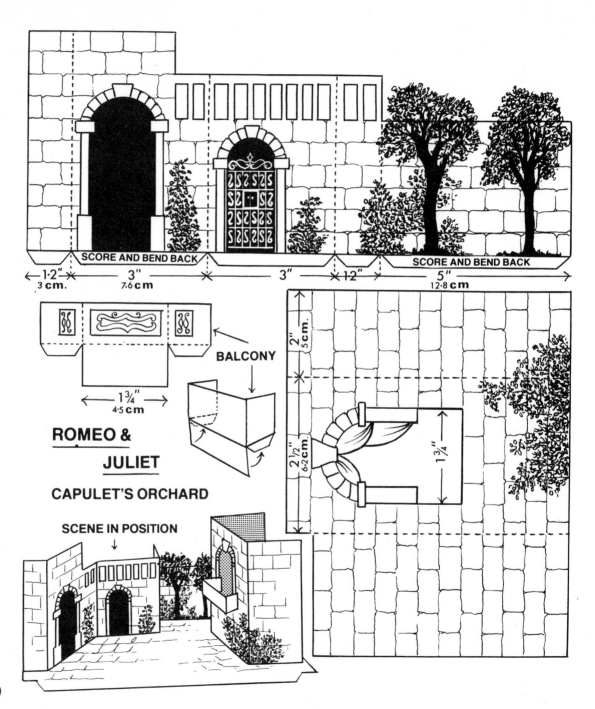

SCORE AND BEND BACK

SCORE AND BEND BACK

← 1·2" → 3 cm.

3" 7·6 cm

3"

1·2"

5" 12·8 cm

BALCONY

2" 5 cm.

2½" 6·2 cm.

1¾"

← 1¾" → 4·5 cm

ROMEO &

JULIET

CAPULET'S ORCHARD

SCENE IN POSITION

Fig. 26. Plan view of the setting for *Capulet's Orchard*. There is ample scope here for effective use of colour.

Fig. 27. Photograph of the setting constructed for *Capulet's Orchard*. This can be dropped into place on stage as a complete unit.

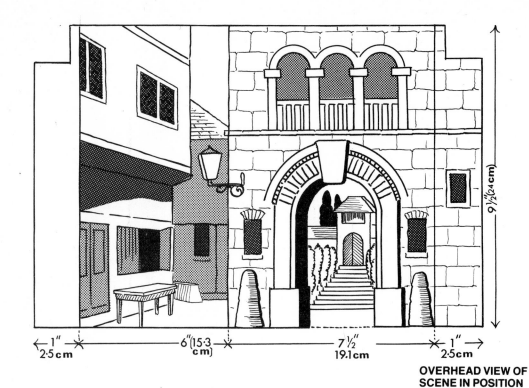

9½"(24cm)

1"
2·5cm

6"(15·3 cm)

7½"
19.1cm

1"
2·5cm

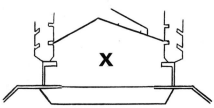

OVERHEAD VIEW OF
SCENE IN POSITION

X

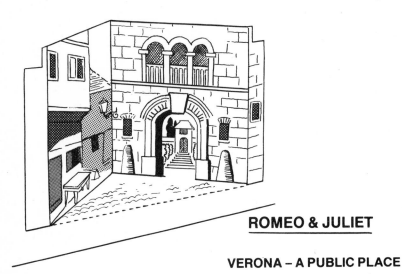

ROMEO & JULIET

VERONA – A PUBLIC PLACE

Fig. 28. The setting for *Verona – A Public Place* illustrates how it is possible to vary the angle of the scenery to achieve different effects. Note also the 'backing' behind the archway.

Fig. 29. The leading characters from *Romeo and Juliet*. Shakespeare's main source of reference for the play was a lyric poem *Romeus and Juliet* written about 1562. The play was published some 35 years later.

Romeo I

Romeo II

Nurse

Juliet

Tybalt

Lord & Lady Capulet

Mercutio

63

CHAPTER 9
THE CIRCUS

Techniques of presenting a
circus: how to construct some
of the performers: the clown,
ringmaster, glamorous girl,
elephant and the rider

It may seem strange to suggest that you should present a circus on your model stage, but in fact this can be done very successfully. If backed with appropriate music it can provide half-an-hour of amusing entertainment.

The technique is quite different from that described in previous chapters, mainly because the characters are jointed and are operated from behind the scenes and not from the wings.

The scene or, more properly, the background, needs very careful preparation and the plan shown in Fig. 30 must therefore be carefully followed. On my model this background is constructed from black card, but the colour is not of major importance, provided that it does not detract from the 'performers'.

Fig. 30 also illustrates, in miniature, a basic selection of circus performers for your very own 'big top'. You can, of course, add any others that your imagination and ingenuity can conjure up. A 'high wire' act would be a challenge for any modeller! Figs. 31, 32 and 33 are actual size working drawings showing the basic construction.

The Clown

I will deal with the construction of this figure (see Fig. 31) in some detail. Decide first of all whether you prefer (a) to work on paper, and afterwards glue the figures onto card, or (b) whether you prefer to trace the figures directly onto card. Ordinary drawing-paper is not strong enough for these characters and I recommend a good quality card of medium thickness as the most practical solution. Having settled this point, trace the various sections onto card, taking care to mark the connecting points very clearly, then cut out the sections. It is a good idea at this stage to take a strong pin and pierce the connecting points in order to ensure that they do not later become obliterated under layers of paint.

You can use paint or Letrafilm for colouring this figure and although I am something of a Letrafilm fan I find that, in this case, paint is more satisfactory. Use strong colours – blue hat, green jacket and orange trousers for example. You can leave the face white, but do give him the traditional red nose of the clown.

To fix the sections together you need a number of small pins. I have a junk box in which I hoard a mass of bits and pieces, including a selection of pins in sizes varying from $\frac{1}{2}$ in (1·25 cm) to 2 in (5 cm) long. For our purpose the $\frac{1}{2}$ in pins are ideal for the job. You can do the connecting with cotton if you wish or with thin wire, but I always prefer to use small pins. You need to bend the heads of these pins and you can do this quite satisfactorily by holding the pin head and about $\frac{1}{16}$ in (1·5 mm) of pin firmly between scissor blades and bending the remainder of the pin downwards – see Fig. 31 (1). This should give you a pin bent as in Fig. 31 (2).

You may at first have some difficulty in forcing the pin through two thicknesses of card but by pushing on the pin head and pulling the pointed end downwards, you should soon be able to do so successfully. When the pin is safely through the sections, fix it in place with a small piece of sticky tape. This keeps the pin in position and also avoids giving yourself a nasty puncture when handling the figure!

Finally take a piece of $\frac{1}{16}$ in (1·5 mm) wire, bend it at one end and, using your sticky tape, fix it at the back of the figure at roughly the same height from the stage as the operating slit in the background.

The Ringmaster

The Ringmaster (see Fig. 32) is quite straightforward and follows the construction of the Clown except for his 'disembodied' head. I have made him into a pompous little man, full of self-importance and very conscious of his heavy responsibility as 'Boss-man' of the Circus ring. His wire control, by the way, must be fixed to the back of his head and not between his shoulder blades as for the Clown.

The Glamour Girl

You may not find our Glamour Girl (see Fig. 32) quite so easy to construct, mainly because of her jointed legs. Extra care is needed when pinning her limbs together; the arms should be fixed *behind* the shoulders, and the lower leg *behind* the thigh. If you decide to use the cloak, complete the figure first and attach the cloak as a last operation.

Elephant

The Elephant (see Fig. 33) is very simple to construct, but he is a most effective and popular character. I have made him plump and chubby – and there is no reason why you should not make him a pink elephant too!

The Rider

The Lady Rider (see Fig. 33) may be a little more complicated, but she is a colourful figure and it is worth taking a little trouble to make her perhaps the most outstanding figure of our circus. Fix your wire control to the back of the rider and do not forget that you will need a piece of wool or card from the bridle to the lady's hand as a rein.

Having completed these five figures you have the nucleus of a typical circus. But do not hesitate to try out other characters. There are plenty of suitable circus figures in the pages of children's books and you should not find it too difficult to animate them.

CIRCUS BACKCLOTH

SCORE HERE

SCORE HERE

11½" (29·2 cm)

OVERHEAD VIEW OF FOLDED BACKCLOTH

2"
5·0 cm

2"
5·0 cm

Fig. 30. Great care must be taken with the backcloth. It must allow sufficient space for the introduction of the performers, yet be strong enough to withstand rough treatment.

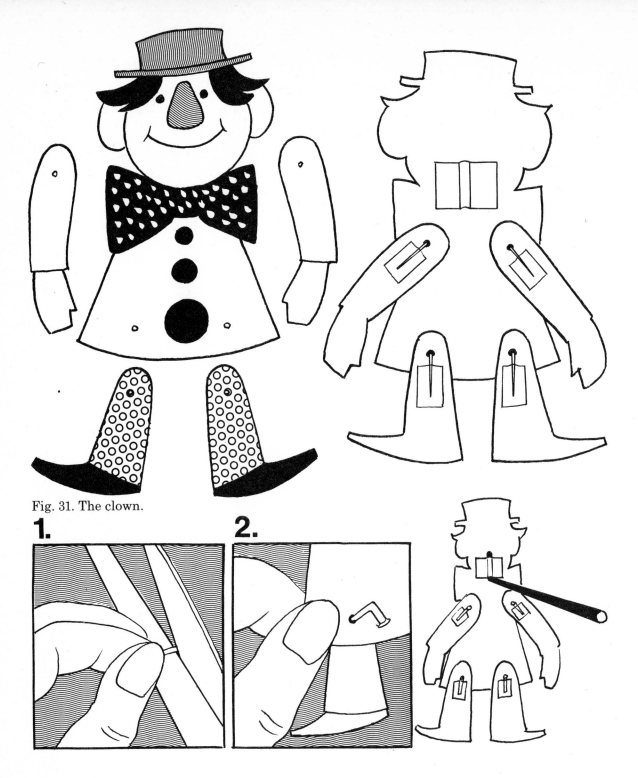

Fig. 31. The clown.

1.

2.

Fig. 32. More circus 'characters'.

SUGGESTED COLOUR SCHEME

RINGMASTER — **COMPLEXION SALMON PINK
COAT & HAT BAND RED   YELLOW FACINGS &
EPAULETS BLUE WAISTCOAT   GREY TROUSERS**

GLAMOUR GIRL

**PALE PINK SKIN   PURPLE CLOAK   LIGHT BLUE
DRESS   BLUE HAT**

COLOUR SCHEME

HORSE – LIGHT FAWN DARK PATCHES

RIDER – **BLUE SCARF WHITE SPOTS RED
SHIRT   YELLOW TROUSERS**

**ADD YELLOW CORD
FROM BRIDLE TO RIDERS
HAND AS REIN**

Fig. 33. You can get a lot of fun out
of these figures.

**COLOUR ELEPHANT
PINK**

**RED
MOUTH**

CHAPTER 10
PRODUCING
A MUSICAL:

The Pirates of Penzance

Staging a Gilbert & Sullivan comic opera: use of the record player: brief synopsis of *The Pirates of Penzance*: some notes on production

After two such totally contrasting forms of entertainment as Shakespeare and a Circus, we will turn our attention to musical comedy. I am assuming that you own – or have access to – a record player or tape recorder and that amongst your records or tapes there will be selections from a popular musical – or, better still, the complete score. If this sort of music is not normally your 'scene' your local record store or library should be able to provide something suitable for use with your model theatre. I know of nothing better for our purpose than the evergreen works of Gilbert and Sullivan and I am proposing to stage *The Pirates of Penzance* simply because I happen to have the complete vocal score, and also because I have 'produced' this Gilbert and Sullivan opera myself on a model stage, without difficulty and with a fair measure of success. *The Pirates* is not quite so well known as *The Mikado*, *The Gondoliers*, or *The Yeoman of the Guard* but it is tuneful, colourful and lively, and presents no major snags to the model theatre producer.

The story is typically Gilbertian. Frederick, a handsome young pirate of 21 has been apprenticed in error to a pirate band by his nurse, Ruth. She, poor misguided woman, had mis-read her instructions: Frederick should have been apprenticed to a pilot!

She confesses her sad story in a song *When Frederick was a little lad, he proved so brave*

and daring. Happily, on reaching the age of 21, Frederick's long apprenticeship is over and as the curtain rises on Act I we see him preparing to leave his piratical chums for a more civilised society.

At this point we are introduced to Major-General Stanley and his bevy of beautiful daughters (about 20 of them!), one of whom, Mabel, falls heavily for the reformed Frederick. The Major-General tells us all about himself in the well known patter song *I am the very model of a modern Major-General*.

While Frederick and Mabel engage in a charming love duet, the girls take off their shoes preparatory to enjoying a paddle.

This idyllic scene is rudely interrupted by the return of the pirates. The girls and their 'papa' are captured by the pirates but are later released by the tender-hearted Pirate King when he learns that the General is – like himself – an orphan.

But in claiming to be an orphan, the General has told a despicable lie and in Act II we find him confessing his guilt to his recently acquired ancestors in his recently acquired ancestral home! He is comforted by Mabel and Frederick, who declares his intention of leading an expedition against his former pirate comrades. Unfortunately for Frederick he was born in a leap year and, as the Pirate

King explains, 'Though you've lived 21 years, yet if we go by birthdays, you're only five and a little bit over!' Frederick, whose incredible sense of duty is almost beyond comprehension, is forced to rejoin his pirate friends and to tell them that General Stanley is, in fact, no orphan – what's more he never was one!

The Pirate King plans a swift and terrible revenge on the General and his daughters, but in one of the 'stagiest' of stage fights he and his pirates are overcome by a posse of policemen. The opera reaches a satisfactory and very Gilbertian conclusion when the old nurse Ruth reveals that the pirates are 'all noblemen who have gone wrong'. So the pirates marry the General's daughters; Frederick marries his Mabel, and the audience departs singing Mabel's theme song *Poor Wandering one.* . . . If, after reading this synopsis you intend to stage this particular musical, I suggest you borrow a copy of the complete opera, words and music, from your library and study it carefully. You will find some very well-known songs, in particular the Major-General's patter song, already mentioned, and the even better known *Policeman's lot is not a happy one.*

An earlier Gilbert and Sullivan opera, *HMS Pinafore*, had been 'pirated' by a number of enterprising American producers, and simultaneously with the London run, five New York theatres were presenting highly Americanised versions of the opera to packed houses. No international copyright was in force at that time and the New York theatre managers were well within their legal rights.

Nevertheless the irascible Gilbert was furious and even the habitually mild-mannered Sullivan was more than a little annoyed. Then impresario D'Oyly Carte had a brain wave. Why not present the first night of a Gilbert and Sullivan opera in New York? That would be quite a sensation and would certainly beat the American 'pirates'. So the Fifth Avenue Theatre in New York was booked and the partners set sail for the States, with most of the music and libretto of *The Pirates of Penzance* in their luggage. Then began a real theatrical 'cloak and dagger' operation.

The first step was to present the authentic version of *HMS Pinafore* at the Fifth Avenue Theatre: this was rapturously received by New York audiences. At the same time preparations were quietly going ahead for the premiere of *The Pirates*. No firm details were given to the press but one or two tantalising snippets were cunningly 'leaked', and on New Year's Eve 1879, before a fashionable New York audience the curtain went up on *The Pirates of Penzance*. Immediately the American 'pirates' went into action. They took shorthand notes of the libretto and did their best to coerce, bully or bribe the members of the orchestra to hand over the band parts. But G & S had been too clever for them. A few

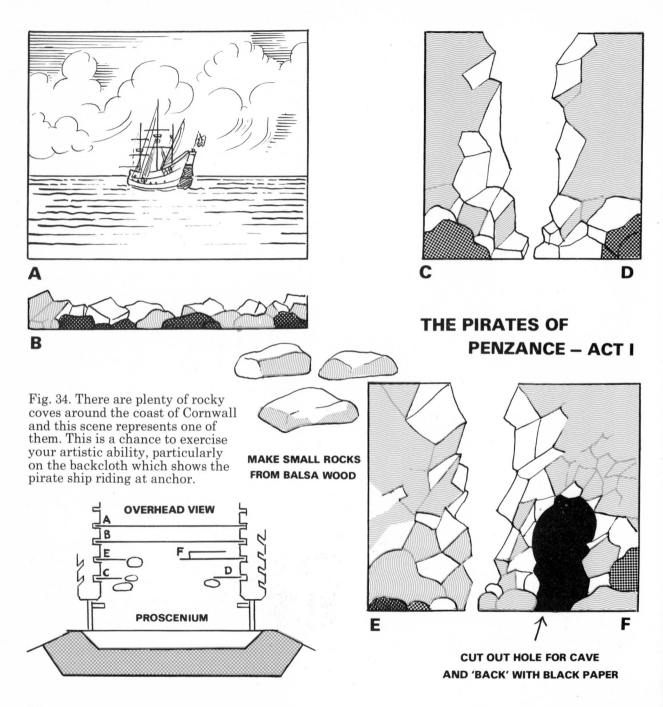

A

B

C

D

THE PIRATES OF PENZANCE – ACT I

Fig. 34. There are plenty of rocky coves around the coast of Cornwall and this scene represents one of them. This is a chance to exercise your artistic ability, particularly on the backcloth which shows the pirate ship riding at anchor.

MAKE SMALL ROCKS FROM BALSA WOOD

OVERHEAD VIEW

A
B
E   F
C   D

PROSCENIUM

E   F

CUT OUT HOLE FOR CAVE AND 'BACK' WITH BLACK PAPER

hours before the New York première *The Pirates* had its first British performance at the tiny Royal Bijou theatre at Paignton, Devon to an audience of about fifty people. This procedure was sufficient to establish British copyright and it was adopted for all subsequent G & S operas.

Incidentally, Gilbert had a toy theatre in his London home and for the *Pinafore* setting he actually constructed a half-inch scale model of the deck of a warship and used small blocks of wood to represent the characters.

Producing 'The Pirates'

I have prepared a design for Act I of *The Pirates of Penzance* and this is illustrated in Fig. 34. This rollicking Act is set in a rocky cave in Cornwall with the pirate ship riding at anchor in the bay.

I do not see any need for making an elaborate set – a backcloth, a line of low rocks and two sets of wings should be sufficient, but if you wish you can add a few extra rocks of grey-painted balsa wood. Cut pieces of balsa roughly to shape and finish them with emery cloth. Balsa wood is very absorbent so you may need two coats of paint. If you decide to include these extra rocks I suggest you lay a flooring of yellow paper to simulate sand. You can then glue the rocks in position.

The opera's principle characters are all illustrated in Figs. 35 and 36. There are three magnificent male parts in *The Pirates*: the Pirate King himself – on the surface a ruthless ruffian, but, I suspect, with a heart soft as butter; Major-General Stanley, who does not hesitate to lie when it suits him; and, of course, the Sergeant of Police. The other leading characters are Samuel, the Pirate King's First Lieutenant; Frederick, the Slave of Duty; Ruth, a piratical maid of all work; and Mabel, Frederick's girl friend. There is the usual chorus of Pirates, Police and General Stanley's daughters. I have sketched some of these 'supernumeraries' and you can repeat them until you have sufficient figures to complete your cast.

Act II is set in a ruined chapel by moonlight, part of the newly acquired ancestral home of General Stanley, and it is here that the General goes, late at night, to plead with his ancestors for forgiveness for lying to the Pirate King. In this scene the General has doffed his impressive uniform and appears wearing a homely dressing-gown, night-cap and carpet-slippers. His daughters are also in night attire. See Fig. 37.

Fig. 37 also includes sketches for a backcloth and one frontcloth for this Act. If you want a more elaborate scene, simply repeat the front cloth with perhaps a few minor adjustments and make it a three-tier scene instead of two.

This old chapel is presumably in an isolated part of rural Cornwall so we can assume it will be surrounded by plenty of 'greenery'. Make your backcloth a forest of tall trees silhouetted against a dark blue sky. You can either paint the trees with black paint or cut them out of black paper and paste them in position.

The frontcloth consists of part of the old chapel ruins, so try to make them look really ancient with crumbling overgrown masonry.

There is a touching ballad in this act sung to *The River* by the General, surrounded by his daughters in their pretty night attire and each carrying a lighted candle. You should find this both easy and enjoyable to stage, using my sketches in Fig. 37.

Many more ladies and gentlemen of the chorus will be needed if you decide to stage the whole of *The Pirates*, but you should by now be well able to improvise further figures from those I have drawn for you.

Fig. 35. These sketches are of some of the pirate band.

Fig. 36. A grand set of characters all very well known to devotees of Gilbert and Sullivan. The comic policeman is one of Gilbert's most popular creations.

SAMUEL　　　　**SOME OF THE PIRATES OF PENZANCE**

PIRATE KING

MAJOR-GEN, STANLEY

SERGEANT OF POLICE

RUTH

FREDERICK

MABEL

BACKCLOTH

THE PIRATES OF PENZANCE – ACT II

A RUINED CHAPEL BY MOONLIGHT

Fig. 37. You will certainly need to give General Stanley many more daughters, but you can copy my three 'beauties' and simply change the hair colouring.

78

MAJOR-GEN, STANLEY   **MABEL**   **THREE OF HIS DAUGHTERS**

CHAPTER 11
A POP STAR

The sectional model:
animating the figure:
effective miming: some
suggestions for handling the
controls

Show Business does of course cover many forms of entertainment, so you may like to make a special feature of a singer, a comedian, or perhaps an animated Pop Star.

Because there is greater scope for animation and gyration with a guitar-playing pop star, we will concentrate on him for our activated model. The first step is to make a sectional model (see Fig. 38) very similar to those for the Circus. Stick to the bent pin method for joining the various sections together and make absolutely sure that each joint is loose and free. A tight joint will spoil the whole effect. It will be obvious to you that the left shoulder must be fixed *behind* the guitar, as must the legs.

Our pop star must, of course, be able to sing and although it is – so far as I know – beyond our capabilities to make a model figure actually sing, we can, at least, make him mime to a record. Fig. 38 illustrates one way of doing this. Firstly, cut out the marked open mouth and on the reverse of the head glue three pieces of extra thick card (if necessary laminate two pieces together) one on each side of the mouth and one at the base – this latter will act as a 'stopper'. Next glue a piece of thinnish card, of the same texture and colour, if possible, as the pop star's complexion and cut it to fit comfortably between the side pieces. In the centre at the top, fix a length of stiff thin wire (the sort florists use for flower

arrangements). Slot this piece of card between the mouth and the black 'backing' card and, providing it moves freely, you can make your pop star mime most effectively to music from your record player.

To animate the figure itself, fix strong black cotton to the points indicated at one end, and glue or tie the other ends to a piece of $\frac{1}{4}$ in (6 mm) square wood so that the entire figure, plus the controls, is no higher than the background.

To make the background you should follow the design of the Circus backdrop, but without the side and background control slots. In the centre of this background, or immediately above wherever you decide to position your pop star, cut out a rectangle slightly wider than the space occupied by the five controls and deep enough to take your finger and thumb. This will enable you to control the figure from behind, without needing to crane over the front of the stage to see if he is behaving to your satisfaction. It will help (if there is sufficient space), to fix a small label at the side of each control indicating its function – *left arm*, *right arm*, etc.

Finally, glue two small pieces of card on either side and at each end of the control stick. You can then clip it over the background, leaving your hands free to animate the figure.

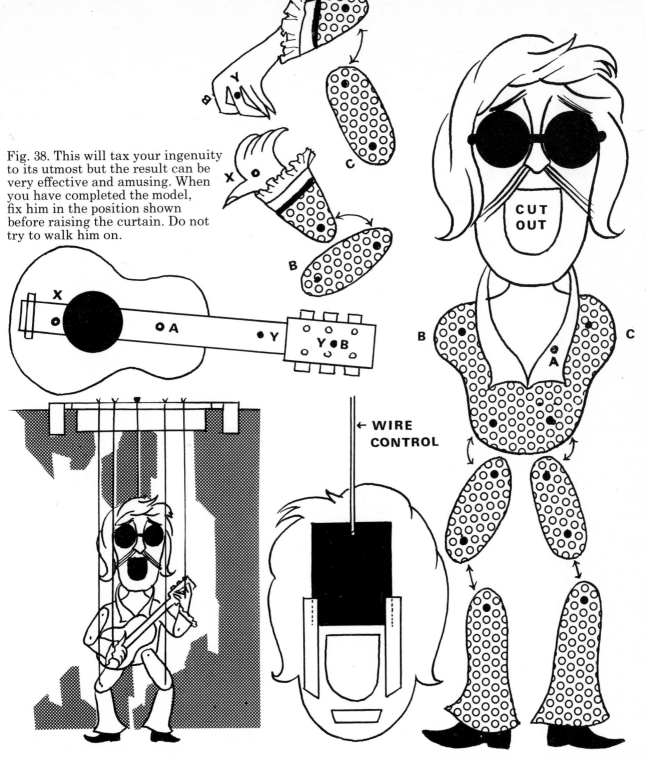

Fig. 38. This will tax your ingenuity to its utmost but the result can be very effective and amusing. When you have completed the model, fix him in the position shown before raising the curtain. Do not try to walk him on.

CHAPTER 12
THE BALLET

Background notes: the Pop-up
theatre: *The Sleeping Beauty*:
How to design and fit the
scenery: the characters

We have now dealt with: the staging of a straight play, a circus, a musical and a pop star. Now let us turn our attention to another important facet of the entertainment scene – the ballet.

Ballet is an art form which combines music, literature, painting and dancing, and the perfect ballet requires perfect balance between each of these elements.

It is, if you like, an amalgam of the arts. Its popularity can be vouched for by anyone who has ever tried to get a decent seat for a ballet performance at The Royal Opera House, Covent Garden, The Lincoln Center, New York, or indeed, anywhere else where ballet is performed.

The origins of ballet go back many hundreds of years – to Italy where 'balli' were performed mainly in praise of the qualities of some important nobleman or his guests. The performers were essentially amateurs and invariably all the parts were danced by men – even the female ones!

In the late 1400's the French invaded Italy to take over the throne of Naples, and they were so impressed with the quality of the 'balli' performances they saw there that they took this new form of entertainment back with them to France. It was Louis XIV who fostered the idea of ballet and it was this worthy monarch, the Sun King, who really established the ballet by opening an academy for professional dancers in 1672. This explains why the technical terms used in ballet today are French – *arabesque*, *entrechat*, *jeté* and so forth.

Today the art of ballet is international and we can enjoy fine performances in Russia, in London, in Denmark, in Germany, Holland, Canada, Australia and in the United States where the New York City Ballet, formed in 1948 by George Balanchine, is recognised as one of the finest ballet companies in the world. The States is also fortunate in having the Dance Theatre of Harlem, generally agreed to be the world's greatest all-black classical ballet company.

I intend to stage *our* ballet in the form of what I can only describe as a 'pop-up' theatre and if you will look carefully at Fig. 39 you will see what I have in mind. This model is three dimensional yet it folds flat like a book. It is, I must admit, rather elaborate and I certainly have no intention of suggesting you embark on anything quite so complicated for your first attempt.

But even for a fairly simple 'pop-up' model you will need plenty of patience. You will also need a small pair of tweezers – one of those specialised items not mentioned in the chapter on Equipment.

Fig. 39. This type of model theatre gives the modeller great personal satisfaction. It is more difficult to make than the conventional model and therefore calls for patience and ingenuity. When closed it occupies no more space than a birthday card.

The Ballet I have chosen for our model is *Sleeping Beauty*. I could have selected one of the great classical 'white' ballets such as *Les Sylphides* or *Swan Lake*, or even one of the lighter modern pieces such as *Pineapple Poll* or *La Fille Mal Gardée*. But having studied many photographs and after a great deal of deliberation, I felt sure that *Sleeping Beauty* would prove of greater interest and that it would not be too difficult. Moreover it is international – as popular in New York as it is in London or Moscow.

The Sleeping Beauty

Sleeping Beauty is one of the finest achievements of The Imperial Russian Ballet. It is exciting, tender, at times poetical, often grandiose, extravagantly dressed and mounted, and enveloped in Tchaikovsky's glorious music. Yet it was poorly received at its first performance on 2nd January 1890 at the Maryinski Theatre, St Petersburg, one critic dismissing it as 'not a ballet, but a fairy tale, a whole divertissement'. The critics, however, were poor prophets and the ballet swiftly won the acclaim of the general public. The first performance in London was at the Alhambra Theatre in 1921 and it was with this ballet that The Royal Opera House re-opened its doors after the war on 20th February 1946. The Royal Ballet's presentation *Sleeping Beauty* made its first appearance in New York in 1949.

The ballet of *Sleeping Beauty* sticks very

closely to the traditional fairy story. The curtain rises on the court of King Florestan where the nobles and their ladies are celebrating the christening of Aurora, the King's daughter. Five fairies present gifts to the princess and all is sweetness and light until this happy domestic scene is rudely interrupted by the arrival of Carabosse, a wicked fairy (hiss) who, furious at not being invited to the christening, prophesies that on her twentieth birthday the princess will prick her finger on a spindle and die. The Lilac Fairy (cheers!) intervenes to say that Aurora will not die but will sink into a deep sleep, from which she will be awakened only by the kiss of a handsome prince.

Time passes (as it always does) and on Aurora's twentieth birthday four princes arrive to seek her hand in marriage. This is a cue for the *Rose Adagio*, one of the most difficult dances for a ballerina in all ballet. She, poor girl, no sooner completes this dance than she is accosted by an old crone with a spindle, and yes, you've guessed it, she pricks her finger and sinks to the ground apparently lifeless. The dastardly Carabosse has had her revenge!

The princess is tenderly carried away to a floral bower and the Lilac Fairy casts a spell of sleep over the entire scene, clothing the palace and gardens in a forest of apparently impenetrable brambles.

A hundred years pass by and one day handsome Prince Florimund is leading his friends in a hunt through the forest where he meets the Lilac Fairy. She tells him about the unfortunate princess and gives colour to her story by conjuring up a vision of the sleeping Aurora. Infatuated by Aurora's beauty, Florimund persuades the Lilac Fairy to guide him to the princess' resting place: on arrival he valiantly hacks his way through a mass of twig and cobweb to the sleeping Aurora and awakens her with a kiss.

Immediately the sleeping court comes to life and the most elaborate arrangements are made for the wedding of Aurora and Florimund. A galaxy of fairy-tale characters comes to pay homage to the happy couple, including Puss-in-Boots, the White Cat, Red Riding Hood and the Wolf, a Bluebird and many more from the world of make-believe. The curtain falls triumphantly on a scene of splendour and happiness.

This ballet is so liberally sprinkled with 'high spots' that selecting an appropriate scene for our model kept me awake at nights. Should we have Carabosse casting her wicked spell; the prince awakening the princess; the Blue Bird dance from Act III or The Lilac Fairy leading Prince Florimund through the forest. Finally I settled for the high spot towards the end of Act II when the old crone – Carabosse to you – pricks Aurora's finger with a spindle and the princess falls to the ground

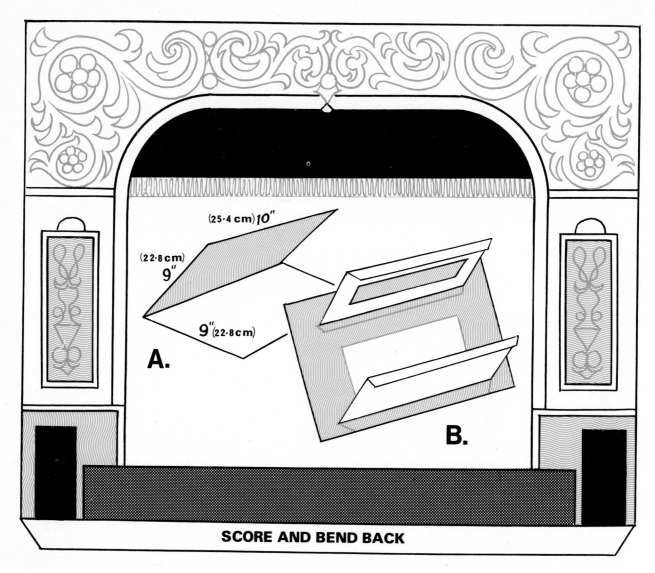

(25·4 cm)10"

(22·8 cm)
9"

9"(22·8 cm)

A.

B.

SCORE AND BEND BACK

Fig. 40. The proscenium for the 'pop-up' theatre. If you follow this design a suggested colour scheme is; fawn background, dark brown base behind the orchestra, brown panels on either side with the design in white.

Fig. 41. The diagrams on page 87 are of major importance. Try to be 'super accurate' when marking out the positioning of the scenery and the figures. A little extra time spent now may save you much frustration later on.

BACKCLOTH – HALF ACTUAL SIZE

4" (10·2 cm)

6½" (16·5cm)

THE SLEEPING BEAUTY

TORMENTORS

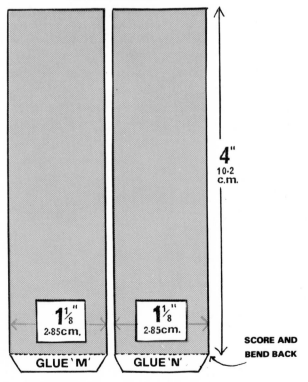

4" 10·2 c.m.

1⅛" 2·85cm.

1⅛" 2·85cm.

GLUE 'M'

GLUE 'N'

SCORE AND BEND BACK

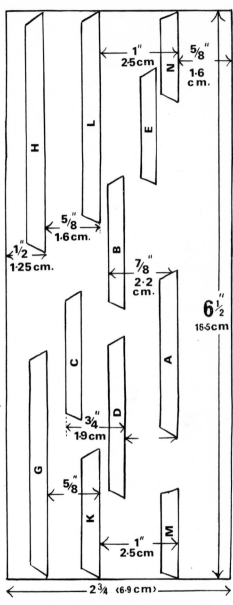

PLAN OF STAGE SHOWING POSITIONING OF SCENERY AND FIGURES

1" 2·5cm

⅝" 1·6 c m.

⅝" 1·6 cm.

½" 1·25 cm.

⅞" 2·2 cm.

6½" 16·5cm

¾" 1·9 cm

⅝"

⅝"

1" 2·5cm

2¾" (6·9 c m)

H L E N B A C D G K M

in a trance. Her old nurse rushes forward in panic while the King and Queen look helplessly on.

In the ballet itself this is a busy scene with the King, Queen, four princes, the ladies and gentlemen of the court and a crowd of lads and lasses of the village. I have tried to simplify the scene and I am confident that it will not be beyond your capabilities.

Construction

Cut out a piece of thick card, 18 in × 10 in (45·5 × 25·5 cm) and score it down the centre so that it folds up like a book (Fig. 40, Diagram A).

Then take a piece of thinner card, and trace or copy the proscenium design I have suggested in Fig. 40. You do not, of course, have to use my design, but even if you prefer to evolve your own, I strongly advise you to follow my dimensions – in this case 7½ in × 6 in (19 × 15·2 cm) with a ½ in (1·25 cm) gluing flap. Colour the design and then cut out the proscenium arch, but keep Fig. 40 Diagram B by you for a little longer.

In this model, the stage platform is of major importance. To make this platform you need a piece of stiff card, 2¾ in × 6½ in (7 × 16·5 cm) with two gluing strips ⅝ in (1·6 cm) deep along each of the longer edges. Mark out this platform exactly as shown on the plan in Fig. 41,

and glue it carefully into place on the back of the proscenium.

The stage will also need a top, so prepare another piece of card 2¾ in × 6½ in (7 × 16·5 cm) with ½ in (1·25 cm) gluing flaps, and cut out a rectangle, 5 in × 1½ in (12·7 × 3·8 cm) to allow for top light. Glue this into position at the back of the proscenium and about ½ in (1·25 cm) down from the top. The back of the proscenium should now look something like Fig. 40 Diagram B.

Next study the plans for the scenery as shown in Fig. 42. These consist of a backcloth; a low wall (in two sections); two wings, one on either side of the stage, but joined in the centre. You will find it an advantage to make and colour all these units at this stage and to fix them in position on the stage platform. At the same time you should make and fix the 'tormentors' (remember them?) on either side of the proscenium. When gluing all these bits and pieces into place stick meticulously to the positions indicated on the diagram. Accuracy is vital.

Now we start on the tricky part. Draw a thin line on the right side of the book, exactly 2¾ in (7 cm) from the centre fold. Glue the proscenium firmly in place along this line. You should now glue the backcloth in place opposite the proscenium and ⅝ in (1·6 cm) from the centre of the book.

THE COMPLETE SCENE

GLUE 'G'

GLUE 'H'

SCORE AND BEND BACK

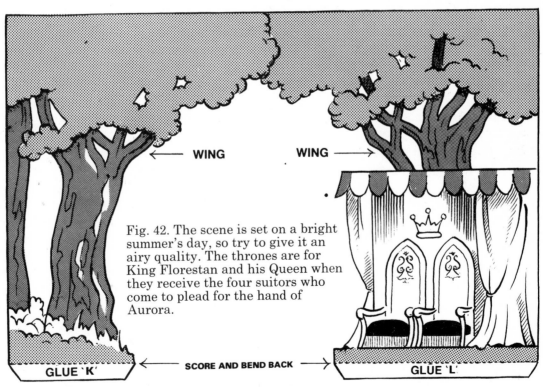

← WING   WING →

Fig. 42. The scene is set on a bright summer's day, so try to give it an airy quality. The thrones are for King Florestan and his Queen when they receive the four suitors who come to plead for the hand of Aurora.

GLUE 'K' ← SCORE AND BEND BACK → GLUE 'L'

The theory behind this 'pop-up' type of model is that every unit, be it scenery or figure, is firmly attached to a unit immediately behind it.

Sounds a bit crazy perhaps but let us take one section of the low wall and apply the 'pop-up' principle to it.

Cut a piece of stiff card, about $\frac{3}{4}$ in (1·9 cm) long and exactly $\frac{1}{2}$ in (1·25 cm) deep (to correspond with the distance of the wall from the backcloth). Allow two gluing flaps as in Fig. 43 Diagram Y. Glue one of these flaps to the back of the wall.

Using your strongest glue smear liberally the flap on the back of the platform and the flap marked (Z) on the back of the wall. Allow the glue to become tacky then close the book firmly and press it under some heavy object, or even sit on it for a couple of minutes, to allow the glue to set.

Open the book – and Presto! If all your measurements have been accurate the platform will be fixed in position and the wall upright and parallel to the backcloth.

And that is really all there is to the pop-up principle. Once you have established the method of operation of this single piece of scenery, you should treat the other units similarly, not forgetting the roof.

The main point to keep in mind is that the connecting flaps on the back of each unit match exactly the distance between corresponding units on the stage platform. Do not fix these flaps too high or you may foul the roof.

You will find that fixing the scenery units separately is a rather tedious performance so, if you wish, you can try and make one operation of it by smearing glue on each flap and then going through the same routine as for the wall.

After completing the stage and scenery to your satisfaction you are ready to start on the dancers, who are illustrated, actual size, in Fig. 43. Trace these figures on thin card, colour them suitably, and cut them out.

Use plenty of bright, rich colour. Courtiers of those days had money to burn and never stinted themselves on clothing. Silks, velvets and elaborate brocades were the order of the day for both ladies and gentlemen of 'quality' and in fact the 'peacocks' often outdid the 'peahens' in finery. Having coloured the figures to your satisfaction, score and bend the base flaps, and note carefully the position of each group on the stage.

Fix connecting flaps on the back of these, colour them suitably, and cut them out. Score and bend the base flaps and note carefully the

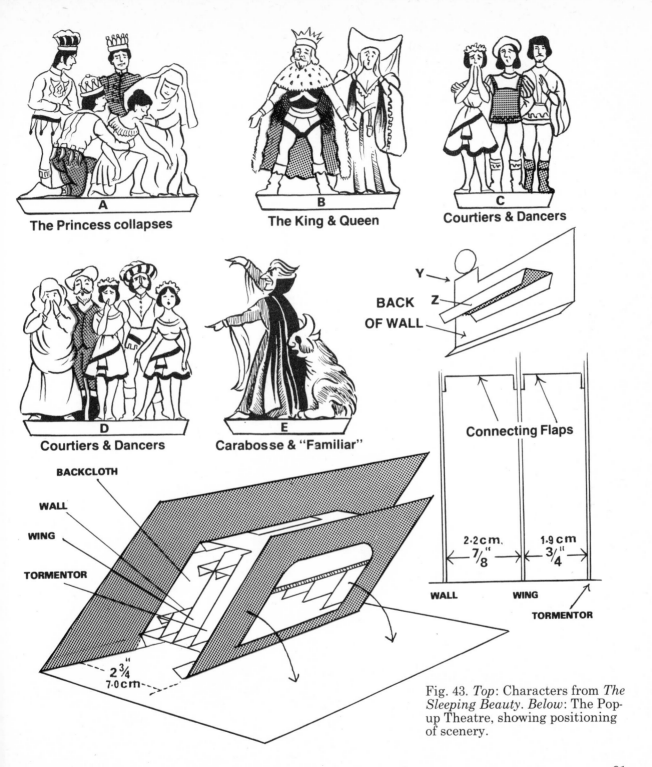

A The Princess collapses

B The King & Queen

C Courtiers & Dancers

D Courtiers & Dancers

E Carabosse & "Familiar"

Y

Z

BACK
OF WALL

Connecting Flaps

2·2 cm.
7/8"

1·9 cm
3/4"

WALL

WING

TORMENTOR

BACKCLOTH

WALL

WING

TORMENTOR

2 3/4"
7·0 cm

Fig. 43. *Top*: Characters from *The Sleeping Beauty*. *Below*: The Pop-up Theatre, showing positioning of scenery.

position of each group on the stage. Fix connecting flaps on the back of these groups, checking that they are of the right size for attachment to the unit or figure immediately behind them. You will find that the stage layout is planned so that all units are interconnected. Try and fix the dancers simultaneously – it is much more satisfactory than treating them individually. If you have difficulty in gluing the figures in place, use your tweezers; they are particularly useful at this stage. It can be very frustrating trying to handle the smaller pieces with your fingers which, at such times, seem to swell to twice their normal size.

Do not expect to achieve complete success with your model at the first attempt, unless of course, you are either very lucky or particularly skilful. It could be that you will have to detach some of the units and re-glue them. Do not let this bother you as with patience and perseverance you will soon be producing pop-up models of many things, and not necessarily theatres.

And incidentally, I almost forgot that you might perhaps like to add an orchestra to your pop-up model. Nothing easier! Trace, colour and cut out the lines of musicians in Fig. 44 and fix them in position, using exactly the same technique as for the theatre itself.

Finally, Fig. 45 is a photograph of *The Sleeping Beauty* constructed entirely from the drawings and explanations given in this chapter. The picture is only in black and white, but at least shows that it can be done!

SCORE AND BEND BACK

SCORE AND BEND BACK

SCORE AND BEND BACK

Fig. 44. The final touch to our
'pop-up' model – the orchestra.
This is not absolutely essential
but it is a thoroughly worthwhile
embellishment, especially when
staging a ballet. It is the music
coupled with colour and movement
which makes the ballet such an
entrancing form of entertainment.

Fig. 45. The completed model of the
'pop-up' theatre.

RING UP THE CURTAIN

Having taken the trouble to build a model stage do not, I beg of you, put it to one side and forget it. Put it to work – use it and enjoy it.

In this book I have indicated all the varied possibilities the model theatre has to offer. To the professional or keen amateur actor, producer or designer, its uses are obvious and there have been – indeed still are – many well-known impresarios who have designed and planned many successful productions on their own model stages.

Do not be content to limit your model to the forms of entertainment I have described. They are intended only to illustrate four totally dissimilar ways of using it. Experiment a little: try staging a modern straight play for example, or one of the famous period pieces such as *The Importance of Being Ernest*. The

'scripts' can usually be found in bookshops or in your local library.

If you find that you are really 'hooked' on the model theatre as a hobby you may want to extend your model by installing a lighting system. This is not particularly difficult, but unless you know something about electricity you must get help from someone who does. Even a very simple system of lighting can make a model so much more interesting to operate. If you want to be really ambitious, try to get hold of a 'dimmer' for the footlights. Then you can simulate that exciting moment when the house lights dim, the footlights glow and the audience waits in silence for 'curtain up'.

In the modern theatre a team of very important people is needed to stage a play.

Success or failure depends very largely on the Director. He is responsible for casting the play, conducting rehearsals, or exercising overall control of stage management and even for dealing with the tantrums of the leading players! His job must not be confused with that of the Producer who is mainly concerned with the business side of the production.

The Director, unless he is a superman, cannot possibly hope to cope with every job himself and in all major productions he can call on the services of such experts as the stage manager, the scenery and costume designers, lighting engineers, carpenters, painters, the wardrobe mistress, prompter and 'props' manager. If it is a musical, a Musical Director is of course essential.

Very few productions can afford to employ all these specialists and usually some doubling-up is necessary. Often some of the less exacting duties will be taken on by an aspiring young actor or actress. Many of our 'stars' of today will freely admit that they learnt their craft by serving as ASM (Assistant Stage Manager) at some provincial theatre.

Gordon Craig – one of the 'greats' of theatrical history – once said that 'the ideal artist of the theatre is the man (or woman) who can write the play, direct the actors, design the set and the lighting and provide any other element that may be needed'. A tall order indeed and one which very few people have been able to satisfy. But you, with your model theatre, have every chance of fulfilling most of Gordon Craig's conditions, except perhaps writing the play. And who knows, you may even be able to tackle that!

And now a few hints on presenting the play. First of all, NEVER stage a production 'cold'. In other words, make your preparations well in advance and try to organise a 'dummy run'. Secondly check all your 'sets' and characters and see that they are in proper working order. This may seem obvious but I have seen presentations ruined when some of the 'characters' collapsed on stage.

Thirdly, play some suitable background music on tape or record-player while the audience take their seats. Select music which will put the audience in the right mood.

If you are doing a straight play with 'voices off' do get your 'voices' to speak clearly and not to skimp their words.

Finally – and perhaps the best advice I can give you – *never* lose your temper. However bad things seem, losing your temper will only make them worse.

Now let us 'Ring Up the Curtain'.

INDEX

CREDITS

The author wishes to express his thanks to Mr Ron Harrington, A.I.I.P., and Mr Shaun Trewinnard, who took the photographs; to his secretary, Sheila, for typing and re-typing the manuscript; and to his grandchildren, Simone and Jason, who helped – perhaps unwittingly – in the preparation of this book.

To Alan Folly and the staff of William Luscombe Ltd the author offers his thanks for their help and guidance and for their unfailing tolerance at all times.